*CHAPLIN* : *LAST OF THE CLOWNS*

# chaplin

## LAST OF THE CLOWNS

*by*

# PARKER TYLER

*the*
**VANGUARD**
*press*
*inc.*

# acknowledgments

The author's indebtedness to Mr. Joseph Cornell and Mr. Theodore Huff is great for making available to him their respective superb collections of Chaplin "stills," which yielded all that was necessary to render the points of this story pictorially clear. Specific credit will be found accompanying each illustration.

The author also wishes to acknowledge with thanks his dependence on *An Index to the Films of Charles Chaplin*, by Theodore Huff (Special Supplement to *Sight and Sound*, Index Series No. 3, March 1945) for refreshment on the plot-incidents of Chaplin's movies and for all statistics relating to their issuance.

The quotations from *Charlie Chaplin* by Gerith von Ulm, published by The Caxton Printers, Ltd., Caldwell, Idaho, are used by special permission of the copyright owners. The quotations from Thomas Burke's essay on Charles Chaplin in *City of Encounters* (copyright, 1932, by Thomas Burke), are reprinted by permission of Paul R. Reynolds and Son, 599 Fifth Avenue, New York, N. Y.

**to** THE GREATEST ESTHETE IN FILM

*sergei m. eisenstein*

# illustrations:

## illustrations

# CHAPLIN : LAST OF THE CLOWNS

# I *the* *caricature* *of a man*

**one**  The very young child is the natural aristocrat. When first he enters the world, he is slapped. This slap serves merely to draw his attention, to fix it on the objectivity of existence. Thereafter, all basic fears (which even an aristocrat eventually has) are subordinated to the effect of the apparent conspiracy to give him delusions of grandeur. He is a magnetic center into which all kinds of loving attentions are plunged, dipped, insinuated.

We know the legend of "the youngest," the

baby of the family, whose existence, even before his own wish, is "law." Truly, in the case of the average human infant, he is not at all his own master since he is more or less a domestic, a nursery, commodity; a bundle to be passed here and there, outlawed from one place at the tick of a clock, established in another at its tock.

But has the child any conscious wishes or preferences at this stage? Well, he is often hungry and at short notice. Adults little realize the agony, even of seconds, imposed on a hungry child, the craving of whose stomach knows no law or order; it simply *is*.

The least frustration is a baby trauma to the desiring infant. Then there are the true traumas, which lie in ambush, ignominiously. First there is the trauma of birth itself, the difficulty of being born, that great original ambush. Then the inevitable trauma: the other "first slap" that the child is capable of orientating, of ascribing to the agency of the world—to that thing outside.

But think of the innocence!—no, I mean the *ignorance;* for "innocence" has a theological tinge. The child is the opposite of innocent. Every tangible experience leaves its mark, however slight. But in a very unsystematic fashion. The well-being of the properly cared for child can produce only those intuitions of security and poise that distinguish the demeanor of the aristocrat, bland assumer of well-being. It is an implicit knowledge, a knowledge that takes the harmony of existence, the abundance of the world, for granted. It is, from the infantile viewpoint, an automatic reciprocity to what seems foreordained.

The conspiracy of benevolent parents and nurses is to gratify every little wish the child comes to have. And to deny a child—because he annoys us by crying or just out of the artless, automatic sadism that even parents have—what is this? It is only to initiate desire into being the *passion* of desire, to give it growth at the root, so its flowers shall rage at their will. To gratify after teasing: this is to teach the child that the inevitability of ends is enriched by suspense. Thus the discipline that "modern" parents dream of imposing (though now in child-rearing, of course, there is a modern anarchy) is merely another instrument by which the child constructs his willy-nilly aristocratic premise of existence.

Regularity and rule for the infant are more important than inspiration, for as yet the child cannot invent for himself, he can only learn the facts. Yet "the facts" are the loaded dice perpetually supplied by adults. The dice of infantile education are invariably protean with assurances of security, of normal wish fulfillment. Hence, even the difference between the sexes, the identities of individuals, are secondary to a pristine arrogance, the logical arrogance of the primacy of self-indulgence.

The infant self is created systematically by the measured satisfactions of average child-rearing; as certain, as eternal, as the seasons. Only late does he distinguish mother from father, nurse from mother, bottle nipple from fleshly nipple; only late, here from there, self from another, the finite from the infinite. He lives in an aristocratic infinite slowly being transformed into a plebeian finite. But the transcendent irony of the ego may well prevail. Such knowledge, coming only gradually and as though from behind a complicated bulwark of mottled light and dark, serves to define— as the space of a room is defined by the objects in it—the nature and special character of *the given realm*. "The given realm" is what?

**18**

. . . Ideally, to the ignorant but passionate, esthetic gaze of the infant—what but the kingship of man, the gifts at the foot of the manger?

**2** Before this perspective of the child as aristocrat, I want to erect the world image of Charlie Chaplin, whom, in the light of his history, I call "The Last of the Clowns." The preceding section is like the vague, suspect news of a comet—that astronomical freak. The comet has actually come. It has gone. Chaplin's epic of the child aristocrat, the great artist, and the frustrated lover, has taken place. It has achieved, in its passage, a kind of climax: a logic of development, crisis, and resolution. And it has its peculiar character, its specific, unique conditions. These I propose to set forth.

**3** A biographer of Charles Chaplin, Gerith von Ulm, has said of the boy of five: "The whole modelling of the head on

**19**

the undersized, frail body is old and self-reliant—
a challenge to standardization, the accustomed
order." A "challenge" because, in early childhood,
the aristocratic order was negated by poverty. As
in most beings in whom genius sprouts, a certain
anticipation of the end is contained in the beginning. The adjective "old," the key term of the
foregoing quotation, is far from being a piece of
impressionism. Children who exhibit precocious
intelligence of any kind strike their elders as
"adults"; that is, like themselves. There are, moreover, boys who begin by being referred to, either
from parental wish or simple reaction to the child's
unusual proclivity, as "little men." Chaplin may
not have been such a little boy; he became, however, such a little man.

His father was a handsome person with the profession of music-hall comedian. He was Mrs.
Chaplin's third husband and is described by Miss
von Ulm as "gentle and music-loving." Assuredly,
this is precisely what we would expect in a precursor of the clown whose face, when his heart
was touched, took on that sublime expression
which is the dubious, popular image of someone
listening to music—someone lifted to the heights

—a "true music-lover." To be a music-lover is distinct from being a musician, a composer, or a music critic; to be "music-loving," in the laconic sense of that epithet, is virtually to be equated with the humane on so ordinary a level that thereon every problem tends to be solved at the first sound of a melody. To be "gentle" as well is perforce to acknowledge that sensitivity that goes inevitably with a certain type of natural well-being; possibly, one might say, of an uncritical well-being, a quasi-aristocratic euphoria. For Charles Spencer Chaplin, Sr., coming on hard times in his profession, became disheartened, took to drink, and shortly thereafter died.

Charlie's father was an evidently mild and unintellectual man; not a thinker in the serious sense. What varieties of human trial, in the family of a broken-down professional who takes to drink, may exist behind a curtain of ignorance is open to only a slight margin of conjecture. But the precise gestures in the comedy of sorrow are not important here. The past of Charlie's life can be used for only one purpose: to fill out the patterns self-evident in the great epos which he has contributed to the history of the clown, and to help substantiate what may seem more or less theoretical in this epos as I shall reveal it. So: there was a gentle, music-loving father who died of drink when the lad was about five. And who was a comedian.

When Mrs. Chaplin found the going too hard, she took the two boys, Charles and his brother Sidney, to an orphanage, one of the "work-'us" schools. Here, assuredly, was a complication of whatever incipient attitude the young artist may have possessed; the father-rival had failed in his duty through what must have seemed, even to his five years, a deliberate choice: drink rather than art. This art (we are told by Miss von Ulm) was already established in the youngster by his mother, not his father, as the art of pantomime. In the London slum where the family lived, Mrs. Chaplin would interpret the private lives of their neighbors by analyzing their demeanor in the street. Mimicry's first motive is unquestionably the double-barreled one of envy and boast: we imitate (first as children) both what we would be (at least secretly) and what we are glad we are not.

So we find that the oversize shoes and the idiosyncratic shuffle of Charlie's clown originate

*caricature*

from those of a cabby in the Kennington district
where the family lived. No doubt, a towering
cabby; and indeed, actually an *old* one. One who
could flourish a whip and drive off smartly—to
who knows where? The oversize shoes were thus,
to little Charlie, like the seven-league boots of
fairy tale fame; and truly, to someone near the
ground, they had the enlargement of perspective:
a purely illusory perspective, like those melodra-
matic close-ups that hotel managements still re-
produce of their hostelries, falsely exaggerating
their eminence and extent. As a matter of fact, if
we start with the shoes of the tramp, Charlie, go
to the baggy pants, and proceed to the jacket and
vest, blousy at the waist, narrow under the arms,
then to the head, elongated by the high forehead
and the derby sitting too high on top, we have a
simple quantifying of natural perspective, incon-
sistent with a *trompe-l'oeil* effect on a flat plane
only because Charlie's head is rather too large for
his slight shoulders. What is this image, thus
viewed as more or less duplicating perspective,
but a paradigm of the adult as seen by the child
near his feet and looking up at the envied height?
Indeed, the derby itself is conspicuous because it

**23**

is a device to increase height. Yet just because the image of Chaplin the adult, as the tramp clown, is so childlike, the illusion of the derby defeats itself, since it tends to minimize the figure beneath it.

It is not insignificant that the top of the derby resembles a balloon: that which rises. Little Charlie felt he could rise toward the adult quickly, magically. At last free of the orphanage and opening the doors of cabs to theatergoers, Charlie exploited the art he regarded as his: the pantomime of mimicry. He made the rich adults laugh and earned tips. This was a power that could have been only an extension of pleasing his mother by like performances. In such performances for his mother, especially after his father's death, he was presumably taking his father's place with an action which he must have thought of as substituting for his father's ability to earn a living for the family. The *depth* of such artistry is attested by Miss von Ulm's anecdote that, following his father's funeral, he did an imitation of his mother at the scene and made his brother laugh. We must assume that this behavior of Charlie's was to some extent a mere reaction to insupportable tension, an emotional letdown.

But it was also more. His mother's grief must have been sheer, absolute; an annihilation of all that's made to a black thought in a black shade. Yet, young as he was, this very expression of feeling seemed essentially in contradiction to his assumption that *emotion* was comic emotion; emotion, as it were, caricatured for the purpose of provoking laughter and amusement. So his mother's grief likewise entered the domain of the comic epos: the realm of the fun-making gesture. Likewise, it was "comic emotion" that he connected with earning money. One cannot help thinking, here, of the deliberate offense of the young James Joyce at his mother's deathbed, when he refused, against her urgency, to pray for the peace of her soul. For Chaplin, his own act, wholly positive, was doubtless also a form of irreverence, a diabolic mockery of his mother's grief and the serious significance to all of them of his father's death. Diabolic *and* angelic, because its motivation was certainly an innocent boast that mother and boys were left alive, could move and laugh and love life. Still, doubtless, Charlie felt in his little heart the guilt of feeling, not his mother's grief, but instead a relief that his father's down-

**25**

grade failure had at last reached its climax.

So Charlie's adult tramp, the little man with the unreal mustache and the fabulous courtesy, was a caricature by virtue of *two* kinds of perspective: an actual, or visual, perspective, as we have seen, and what Kenneth Burke terms a "perspective by incongruity," in this case an incongruity of emotion. Charlie's act of mimicking his mother's grief might be considered an outrage; at all events, a piece of childish audacity, full of an astonishing independence. Just because a child is a natural aristocrat, any fragment of genius, large or small, takes root in him and grows into a sword: a magic sort of sword, virtually a wand. Genius is a token of the power to transform what is objective into the subjective style of ease and superiority, the "style" of the infantile experience that genius does not forget and knows how to interpret. Charlie early mastered the kinesthesia of arrogance and poise; a kinesthesia lacerated but never uprooted.

The aristocrat's whim theoretically subjects the world to itself. This is no more than a common tradition that we see illustrated in fairy tales as well as in authentic history: the king's desire.

*caricature*

What is Aladdin's Lamp but the symbol of genius itself, the thing which controlled a genie? Numerous hero geniuses have had their peculiar signs, usually a disfigurement; sometimes it is a hunchback, as with Alexander Pope, or a limp, as with Lord Byron. But this flaw is only symbol of a disability that some prodigious attribute is destined to overcome, to overcome to such a degree that the "normal" is quite surpassed. It is a law of excess compensation. Sometimes it is more an artifice than a physical trait, more exclusively a kind of symbol. Napoleon—a figure which Chaplin has always wanted to recreate on the screen—had his lock of hair: Chaplin, his mustache; Napoleon, his hand thrust into his bosom: Charlie, his cane planted precariously on the ground. Charlie was short as a boy, is short as a man, but his flexible cane was sign of an abstract, sliding scale . . . it was also a wand . . . and Charlie was also "big."

Every child wants to be a man through power at the very moment that he wills to be a child through privilege. The adult aristocrat is one who observes no line of demarcation between power and privilege. Through genius, the child becomes

**27**

the man, *is* the man before anyone can more than guess at the truth. The size and flexibility of Charlie's bamboo cane is deceptive; its very bend-ableness is its attribute of power. If it bent as Charlie walked, it was, to a degree, too long for him, made for a taller man. But he managed it because it *could* bend.

The chameleon quality of the artist and, above all, of the actor-artist, has long been thought of as his peculiar trait, the testimony of his "inno-cence," his lack of responsibility to sincere or "ethical" emotions. However naïve this view, it has an element of truth. The artist, because of his high intuitive content, his extreme emotional charge, places the ambivalence of the emotions before any other quality of life. And especially so because the tour de force of change from tears to gladness, from smiles to grief, tests the flexibility of his art, and because, inevitably, the actor finds moments in his literary material where the drama-tist has daringly, pointedly, juxtaposed comedy to tragedy, literally showed the human face smiling through its tears.

We know there are tears of joy, like Lear's on finding Cordelia, as there is laughter of grief, like

**28**

*caricature*

Rigoletto's on beholding Gilda's head emerge from
the sack. So there was Charlie's comic pantomime
—something with a grimly realistic dimension—in
ambiguous mimicry of his mother's grief. The cane
must be regarded as symbol of this gracile unre-
liability, this deceptive bend and this deceptive
slimness, wielded so artfully by one old before his
time and thus "old" in skill.

An *emotional trompe-l'oeil* was once supplied
by Charlie in one of his earliest screen comedies
when, presumably overcome with grief at his
wife's death, his back shaken as with sobs, he
turned around to face the audience with a cocktail
shaker active in his hands. The sudden inversion
of feeling, produced by the uncovering of a deception as well as by his own unpredictable and
irrational change of mood, became one of the
most inspired features of Charlie's comic art.

We can understand, then, the paradoxical mood
in which Charlie impishly assumed the "mailed
hood" of the artist at the first major emotional
crisis in his life. In the long perspective of his
career, this action may be viewed as a profoundly
defensive measure. By a strange coincidence,
Charlie's surname is derived from the French of

**29**

*capeline,* which means "mailed hood"—think of the hoodlike derby-top! This image, with canes rather than swords crossed beneath it, would do for Chaplin's coat of arms. It is his knightly reply to the overwhelming burden of human emotion, something that he bore like a shield into the battle of his life, which from the first he felt to be largely a *professional* battle: the simple struggle for livelihood.

4 Thoroughly fused in the image of Charlie I have so far projected are the child (the *old* child), the aristocrat, and the artist. Skill in manipulating the cane is closely akin to skill in wearing the paraphernalia of the tramp, in maneuvering the bulky shoes and wearing the flapping pantaloons, which Charlie did with perfect éclat. The incongruity of visual perspective entails as much tour de force in the actor's mechanism as does the incongruity of emotional perspective. The wardrobe of the tramp had to be coherent as the clothes of a living, gesturing, walking, running being. The derby seemed

*caricature*

perched more precariously than it was; moreover, it was a "trick" derby—Charlie could make it perform its own salutation. Thus it is an object of legerdemain, emblem of illusion in accordance with the cane as magic wand. Nothing, generally speaking, could seem more inutile a "fighting organism" than the curious confection that Charlie was if viewed as a pile of old clothes. The little person "inside" the paraphernalia seemed there only by some sort of coincidence, and yet it is not at all surprising that this assortment of ill things had a will to hold itself intact at all costs, and that the astonishing face, so much like a little boy's, was that of a man with extraordinary re. sources, both as a gentleman who doesn't want to be mussed up and as a man capable of defending his honor.

How well we know the image of Charlie in flight—turning a corner somewhat like a sailboat, frantically holding onto his hat and pivoting on the immobile axis of one foot, while the other leg, lifted high and bent, poises for the next stride, with the hand holding the cane at arm's length to maintain balance. The eyes start out with terror beneath the already terrified brows; the mouth seems insignificant, lips pressed diminishingly together under the black, symmetrical patch of the mustache . . . Charlie shows no fight, no chivalry, no dignity now.

Of what is this kinetic image so eloquent a symbol if not the child in the headlong flight of guilt, the child caught red-handed and fleeing for its safety? As to what the crime might be, we have endless archives in which to delve and decide. But in this individual case, it does not matter. Any crime will do. We may be sure, however, that the issue is one to do with guilt before the parent as judge and punisher. But Chaplin, veritably as the adult tramp, is more than a child: he is man, professional actor, artist.

He is an aristocrat turned inside out, a knight turned clown. Yet, although visually, from the child's viewpoint, he is a caricature of a man, he is also, in his moments of humiliating flight, a caricature of the aristocrat; an absolute contradiction of the *child aristocrat* suckled on nursery poise, the aristocrat with a supreme sense of toddling security. This is the child aristocrat's initiation into child serfdom, the first stage of education into being the "technical adult" who must

**32**

shift for himself, even if he be only eight years old
—the age at which Charlie, becoming one of the
"Eight Lancashire Lads," began his professional
career.

So Charlie's flight as the tramp was, both in the
literal and symbolic-retrospective senses, a flight
from the "punishment" of poverty: poverty of
strength or poverty of money, it would be the
same in this light. But let us return to the dis-
graced image of the gentle, music-loving father.

Figuratively speaking, was not the failure of
Charlie, Senior, a sort of *flight*, an escape from
obvious rock-bottom responsibility? Drink was
merely the symbolic coefficient, the symptom. The
parental judge automatically abdicated (as always he must) with the parental provider. The
father's death, then, in a grimly ironic sense, did
become matter for laughter. Out of his very death,
logically, the professional comic triumph of Charlie, Junior, was to arise. This fact little Charlie
glimpsed in one pure stroke of prophetic insight.
How ritual and absolute, then, his mimicry of his
mother's grief! In little Charlie's art, his father's
art was being automatically resurrected.

We find that the image of the fleeing Charlie,

the worsted frightened tramp, is of a triple irony. Supposedly he is in flight from a shameful or at least grievous memory: the defeat of his father in the dual struggle of life and art. Thus, strangely, even as the one who "ran for the green cloth at Verona" in *The Inferno* of Dante, Charlie was winning this race even as he was losing it . . . that is, as his father's memory, incarnated in the tramp clown, was losing it; losing it until Charlie should snatch the cloth like a relay runner and go on to triumph. . . .

Is there not, however, a still further dimension in the "caricature of a man" that Charlie became so early in life? I mean the physical, or visual, dimension. The tramp's sartorial being is a visual perspective by incongruity, the great shoes diminishing to the tiny shoulders; this, as I said, is a caricature of perspective itself. Take this same image in action—specifically, the chaotic motion of wild flight. Subjected to such motion, the symmetry of the dandy, the adult aristocrat, would certainly be distorted, become *asymmetrical*, not only morally, but also visually. Hence, in immobility, Charlie's image as the tramp may be conceived as the equivalent of *perfect proportion*

*submitted to the disorder of helter-skelter motion.*
The perspective illusion represented by Charlie's
costume is therefore a metaphor for the catas-
trophic dishabille of the dandy, adult version of
the child aristocrat. Its movement only underlines
emotionally what it already signifies as a static
symbol: the caricature of a man.

But no matter what happened to Charlie, we
should remember, he never lost his inner, profound equilibrium; this steadfastness was reflected
on the surface by his miraculous "recoveries" of
poise and balance: always the gentleman—and
the more so the more poorly equipped to be. The
image of grace in clumsiness; of articulacy in
inarticulacy. This was Charlie's art of caricature:
an amalgam of the aplomb of an adult with the
awkwardness of a child; or, in a term, *aristocratic
style at any price. . . .*

Even . . . here is the dramatic point, the biographic dimension, the heart of the epos . . . at
the price of earning a living; a price the aristocrat
theoretically, by definition, is never supposed to
pay.

# II
*foundation*
*of the comic*
*epos*

**one**  Both the modern circus clown and the medieval jester, the clown of the royal court, must claim in their planetary lineage the ancient medicine man. It is easy to see how the king's jester, who "physicians" to his master's humors, and who, in Elizabethan plays, uses the word "physic" as a verb, is but a degradation of the witch doctor of African tribes who performed magic cures of all kinds. Moreover, as Rigoletto, jester to Francis II of France, says, "I kill with my tongue." This means that once the

**36**

witch doctor's function was also to slay enemies; later, the jester's wit was to "slay" the affectations and hollowness of the self-seeking court sycophants, the princes, dukes, and lords around the king.

With the evolution of civilized life, the legacy of the great pagan empires, kings maintained personal physicians, who administered to their physical humors, and personal clowns, or fools, who administered to their mental humors. This was simply a division of the total function of the ancient witch doctor. As we view Charlie Chaplin, virtually the last of the true clowns, the ones with genius and personality, we should consider how this division of the witch doctor's labors came to be.

Anthropology proclaims that at one time the triple roles of priest, king, and god were embodied in one individual, and that this individual had the power of healing; thus, he was also a doctor. What this signified is very simple. At this time, in the magic era, mankind believed in an omnipotent being, a manlike creature, who ruled the universe itself, and "doctored" the crops and the weather. Thus, this person was one who held the secret and the power of life and death. Individuals who ruled in the Middle Ages, under the divine-right-of-kings doctrine, were thought to have supernatural power, particularly (as was true of Charles II of England) that of healing by touch. In general, the separation of the three functions of ruling, healing, and conducting rituals (the king's, the physician's, the priest's) has a complicated history. What is important here is the emergence of the clown as a professional wit, the *tragic* symbol of the unseriousness of life.

Clowns in the pagan comedy of Greece were low fellows, virtually feeble-minded, being—like dancing girls—slaves, but their antics had the faculty of amusing in the way the circus clown, and sometimes the vaudeville clown, does today; they were grotesque objects capable of tumbling and other physical tricks frequently of a limited if highly precise genius. Apart from purely theatrical clowns, the masked and dancing mimes, the sign of the clown in the Middle Ages was specifically a hunchback, which he wore as the physical badge of his profession: his mental profession. The Fool in Shakespeare's *King Lear* is the arch example of the philosophic wit of the clown

38

as opposed to the simple-mindedness of Bottom and his pals in A *Midsummer Night's Dream;* indeed, the latter had descended from pagan times and appropriately, therefore, burlesqued the legend of Pyramus and Thisbe.

*Twelfth Night,* in the figure of Malvolio, and *Henry V,* in the figure of Pistol, afford clowns of the aristocratic caliber; that is, low-born fops who affect good breeding and all its perquisites; they are caricatures of gentlemen. Such figures are not far removed from the manner in which Aristophanes lampooned the luxurious style of Agathon in *The Thesmaphoriazusae,* and the last-named character, of course, may be considered a precursor of the well-born fops of Congreve's and Sheridan's comedies, mixing effeminacy and light-mindedness. With Charlie before us, what a strange contrast he provides for all of these, and what a strange likeness. . . .

**2** If the clown, then, as a generic type is *a*) a parody of the aristocratic; *b*) a verbal and pantomimic wit; and *c*) a physical freak of some kind, then he stands in relation to his master, his personal patron, as—in the terminology of modern psychology—an *alter ego:* at once a symbol of conscience and an objective scapegoat for the king's moods. For above all, in the medieval jester's tradition, exists the personal relation of clown to prince. He was his close *confidant,* someone from whom, at his most privileged, the king kept no secrets.

The court clown is not only parody of man in general (being physically grotesque and mentally eccentric) but a particular parody of the king himself in all his aristocratic hauteur. Experience taught the most tyrannical of kings that mundane power has its limits and that life, when all is said and done, is to be concluded with death, with physical annihilation. The jester remains as symbol not only of all the ironies of flattery and disloyalty from the followers of the court but also as an archetypic caricature of all earthly pride and fleshly pleasure; a creature around whom, just because of his flaws and eccentricity, a traditional superstition gathers. Notably, the jester's power, whenever it exhibits itself in history, is diabolic. So, as *alter ego,* he finds himself consistent with

**40**

that ancient unity of witch doctor and king: the heavenly and the hellish in one.

The growth of rationalistic thought undoubtedly must be held responsible for the progressive division of labor which partly accounts for the so-called degradation of the witch doctor into the king's personal fool. The less that religious awe surrounded the vendor of potions (such as the alchemist of the Middle Ages), the more awe accrued to the caste of priests. And, in accordance with the new realism in politics of which Machiavelli was the spokesman, the less awe surrounded the king or prince himself, consequently the more practical and power-minded—rather than superstitious and devout—the prince himself would have to be.

So the Fool became a vestigial repository of magical superstition, the anachronistic crib of the "mental hate" that, in the primitive days of animism, had been considered effective against enemies. The jester became *the symbolic slayer,* whose animistic power was no longer regarded as effectual, but now was confined to verbal and pantomimic witticisms, to the artfully penetrating burlesque. It is not for nothing that, today, a joke

**41**

is termed "killing." Chaplin's latest film, *Monsieur Verdoux,* is such a killing joke.

But the king's jester was no professional clown in the modern sense of the theater. One might say that the circus clown of these times, not a genius of pantomime except in the highest brackets, but only a tumbler and wearer of a grotesque masquerade, is the latest descendent of the one with cap and bells, and that great professional clowns of today are more or less "actors," comedians in the dramatic sense of having solo acts (such as Toodles or Rollins, clowns of traditional motley) or men such as Jimmy Savo, Buster Keaton, the Marx brothers, and Chaplin himself. All the latter, including Chaplin, stem more directly than elsewhere from the Commedia dell' Arte tradition of Pierrot and Harlequin.

The itinerant comedian such as Canio, hero of *Pagliacci,* was a professional whose repertory job was the role of Pierrot, nightly cuckolded by Harlequin with his wife, Columbine. Here two kinds of clown were involved: the foppish clown, Harlequin, with his air of masked romance, "love for a night," and the motleyed or semi-grotesque clown, Pierrot, whose white face is a comic mask

**42**

of grief. The bourgeois is directly opposed to the middle-class dandy. Surely, we may identify Harlequin with Don Juan himself, the immoral philanderer, and Pierrot with the love-bitten, essentially moral Benedict, doomed to betrayal and a broken heart. Charlie's tramp had elements both of the more modish Harlequin and the plainer Pierrot, just as it had (we shall see later) elements of Don Quixote and Sancho Panza. The Pagliacci legend is the link with Charlie's clown and his modern epic, because this legend has the extra dimension of the behind-the-scenes as well as the onstage action of a frustrated love. And this, by a myriad of tokens, has been the situation of Charles Chaplin's love.

**3** So if we look for the epos, or essentially biographic pattern, in the comic history of Charlie, the tramp hero, we find side by side an economic and an esthetic reality; the clown is a professional, a highly successful artist in comedy miming, and a lover whose life

is symbolically reflected by the basically creative
epos of his art. For Charlie the Tramp is a clown
with his individual myth, a story more complex
than the great mass of his admirers can have
realized. First we must recognize that gradually
Chaplin invented a single legend (however varie-
gated in detail) as coherent as Ulysses' voyage
back home. . . .

Invoking the figure of the five-year-old Charlie
just after his father's funeral, in the act of mimicking—in no doubt *silent* gestures—his mother's grief
. . . we see how closely the artist, Chaplin, is
fused with the little man, Chaplin; and how
closely the esthetic problem (naturally involved
with love) is interlocked with the economic problem, the problem of earning a living, that faced
the five-year-old comedian at that very moment.

"The little chap I want to show," Chaplin himself has said of his creation, "wears the air of
romantic hunger, is forever seeking romance, but
his feet won't let him." The grammatical ellipsis
here is as significant as the occurrence of the word
"hunger." Love is a hunger as real as the hunger
of the stomach, and it is these two hungers that
dominate the comic tramp's epos. ". . . his feet

won't let him." Won't let him—what? Apparently, on analysis, won't let him "seek," but as a matter of fact Chaplin has just asserted: "is forever seeking." Certainly the feet don't have to give him their permission *to seek*. What they probably won't *let* him do is "find." Yet how should this come to be?

Possibly we can be confident of uncovering here the missing element of Chaplin's clown, the missing *traditional* element of the Fool's physical and spiritual complexion: the malformation, the *flaw*. The malformation here would be the preponderance of the clown's feet as shown in the tremendous shoes. It is a pedal elephantiasis. We assume that the shoes are *oversize*, but may not this exaggeration be symbolic of the leadenness of the feet, an extra heaviness rather than an extra magnitude? In turn, this unwieldiness, orientated to weight and size (the shoes are doubly in the way of easy performance), may be symbolic of a spiritual quality, just as the jester's hunchback is symbolic of his mental and moral eccentricity.

The feet "seek" but do not "find" because they are too *innately* clumsy, clumsy in feeling as well as in physical accouterment. I have shown how

**45**

the exaggerated proportion of the shoes corresponds to certain illusions of perspective, which in turn reflect the caricature of a man by Charlie the five-year-old boy. Thus it was that, in more ways than one, Charlie inherited his father's shoes too early and had to wear them too early. He also inherited his father's pants, which are included in the caricature of normal perspective. They are also the pantaloons of the grotesque circus clown, a supernatural sort of apparition, as the shoes (likewise the circus clown's) are the esthetic of a preternatural exaggeration, the emblem of a flaw.

Angled toward the circus clown, these symbolic accouterments of dress are more or less fluid, exist in a void without specific reference to life, are mere parts of a surrealistic masquerade. Yet in terms of physical beauty could it not be said of the red bulbous nose of the circus clown that it "won't let him"? . . . What it won't let him do, very naturally, according to the symbolic scheme, would be to find *love*, the so-called happiness of the normal man. For such a nose, if real, would be an uncompensatable disadvantage. Since it is red, it indicates drink: many circus clowns are drunken clowns, and so are the hoboes of the burlesque stage, that rapidly dying institution. It is hardly necessary to recall Chaplin's own upper-class drunks in his early movies. So the clown's red nose would be symbol of a purely moral flaw: drunkenness.

The tramp's shoes have been identified as Charlie's father's by virtue both of personal definition and the abstract science of perspective: boy in relation to man. Psychologically speaking, the very sign of his father's superiority in size could be identified by little Charlie as sign also of his flaw, his drinking, which was inextricably associated with his death. The shoes of the tramp, Charlie, are weighted with the very body of death. They "won't let him" *live.* How is this? They won't let him live . . . as an aristocrat, a nonworker; as the imperial infant. And, in addition, they seem not to let him *grow;* they *root him to the ground,* impede his height.

**4** The line must be drawn between art and labor; between the esthetic and the moral; especially so in the youth of the embryonic artist. The child, if he is the arch aristocrat, is also—and this is a *logical* perquisite of the aristocrat—the arch experimenter, the arch "sampler." The very young artist, one with sure intuition of his genius, delights in nothing more than experience as change and novelty, experience that feeds his increasing sense of the wonder and vitality of existence; his sense of the artless joy and pain of seeking love purely, of seeking absolute love with infinite gestures. And for these "endless" pleasures, there is to be no corollary payment; for the moment, it is only a debt deferred, life having no economic content whatever.

How *esthetic* it was to observe his mother's witty commentaries on their slum neighbors and to mimic these neighbors; how *moral* it was to think of his father's profession as he stood near his corpse, and to mimic his mother afterward. At the very moment when, as I have said, little Charlie symbolically donned the *capeline*, the mailed hood, of his art, he suffered from the burden of its weight, its immediate, ineluctable pressure that entailed, not delirious experiment in the beauty of pantomime (including the pantomime of the lover), but a pantomime whose chief content, at such an age, was its economic power, its money-earning ability. . . . This weight (the mailed hood of art) sank to his feet. Could Charlie not have imagined as an adult, a young man, that somehow this early weight of art, the professional responsibility, "the mailed hood," held him down, prevented his growth, kept him from growing tall?

Displaced, esthetic beauty became economic dowdiness and emptiness, the deceptive derby which the head did not fill. The threat of poverty seemed to bid him seek, but never to let him find. We shall see later how soon this pattern of seeking and not finding—a conspicuously anticlimactic pattern—was established in Charlie's life. In the feet, then, with all the pyrotechnic antics they were to perform, lay the immovable matrix of pain, the phantom of poverty, which somehow—naturally enough—was associated with the pain of love.

*Frustration* became Charlie's professional métier as the clown. And *frustration* is the keynote of all erotic neurosis. Charlie himself said that it was his feet that would not let him. . . . The comic tramp's "gunboats" lay large along the ground. If their horizontal grandeur had been ver-

**49**

ticalized, if they could have raised the tramp's heels, he would have been taller. Height is a great element in male beauty (we must pause to consider) and shortness an obstacle to "romance."

We may speculate that here, in the diminutiveness of stature, is the clown's true, *literal* flaw, of which all the other appurtenances, even the early bamboo cane, the flexible "bladder"—are only symbolic displacements . . . the "comic" flaw . . . "the undersized, frail body" of the boy of five.

5  *Paean.* Charlie of the fresh boutonniere and the soiled vest . . . Charlie of the windy pants, the silent giggle, and the heart of candy . . . Charlie of the boyish mouth and the slim shoulders, of the infant eyes and the Promethean brows . . . Charlie of the outturned toes, open to the blow of fate . . . Charlie of the shuffle, flirt, and skimmer . . . Charlie of the *moue triste* . . . the clasped, terribly normal hands . . . the ten-cent mustache . . . Charlie of the back like a poem . . . Charlie of the

tousled hair, the shrug of the Void . . . Charlie
of the *jeune fille* waist, the feet of a dancer in the
shoes of the earth . . . Charlie, divinely fastidious . . . Charlie of the trick derby, the obliging,
automatic smile . . . Charlie, sad as a vacation-
ing angel . . . Charlie of the heavy date, the hot
romance, the owl's stare . . . Charlie of the epi-
lepsy of tenderness . . . Charlie: credulous as a
dog, suspicious as a cat . . . Charlie, who could
sleep anywhere . . . Charlie of the delicate behind, the straight neck of a prince or a prizefighter
. . . Charlie, the unflagging, mute accusation
against mankind: he of the monosyllabic silhouette . . . of the dash through space . . . the
French kick . . . Charlie, Charlie the funny . . .
Where is he now?—only in the mind, as we remember him, or in the past of "Monsieur Verdoux." . . .

# III

*the clown's*
*triumph and his dream*
*of happiness*

**one** Chaplin's idea of
prosperity, according to Miss von Ulm, who
quotes him directly, was expressed in terms of
"my Turkish carpet and my red lights." He has
apparently never been reticent in admitting that
his first conscious goals were fame and money,
which seem to have been more or less indistin-
guishable in the first half of his career. But this
confusion would be only natural, considering the
commercial standards of the actor's craft. On the

other hand, Thomas Burke, who became Chaplin's friend when the comedian first visited London in triumph, as the star of *The Kid*, wrote an essay on him in which he says, among other revealing things, that Chaplin was not interested in luxury.

It is not—at least it is not *my* concern—that one of the two foregoing versions of Chaplin's temperament should be true and the other false, or that the successful actor, as one used to wealth and bored with it, inevitably outgrew a taste for display or overindulgence. Rather, since I have already erected a figure of him ambivalent at the roots, it must be taken for granted that for every "favorable" aspect of him recorded by observers, almost its exact opposite must also have been recorded.

Thomas Burke's essay is useful in this very respect. "For two hours," he says, "he [Chaplin] will be the sweetest fellow you ever sat with, then without apparent cause he will be all petulance and asperity." Burke also compares the comedian with a "brilliant," a gem, and adds that "the bulk of him is ice." Yet he iterates Chaplin's "essential goodness" and observes: "You have to tell yourself

**53**

that the chubby, well-fed, keen-eyed face is the thin, haggard, bewildered face that you saw in" Charlie's movies. "At no point does the metallic artist in your armchair connect with that forlorn, tousled, futile fool, Charlie." He records the fact that Chaplin invariably refers to the tramp hero as "Charlie," always with the third-person pronoun, "he" . . . tempting one (in the light of the Pagliacci legend) to add the words of the title of Andreev's play ". . . who gets slapped."

**2** I began by referring to the great original slaps—the one provoking the life-reflex at birth and the one serving notice on the child-aristocrat that the world is capable of destroying the state of imperial infancy. Certain words of Thomas Burke's fall into place with these thoughts: "*Charlie* was born full-grown," he says of the tramp hero, the actor's creation. "He lives all his life in the fixed and eternal present of his day of birth." True, one would say, so far as *will* goes; precisely, yes, because the tramp is really a child, as the five-year-old comedian, conversely, was really a man.

Yet Burke adopts the ritual attitude of bewilderment in explaining Chaplin as an artist, being content with this statement: "To attempt to isolate the essence that has placed Chaplin above all other comedians . . . is hopeless." Yet he believes that this "unknowability" of the reason for Chaplin's unrivaled popularity as a world artist is to be explained, perhaps, by the fact that "he is, like so many obscure millions, still the pilgrim, still looking for something without knowing what it is." This was said when Chaplin was at the threshold of his last maturity.

Some natures are completely baffled by the presence of duality, dialectic. Burke is willing to call Chaplin a "spoilt child," to assume that he does not know what he is looking for, to set him at arm's length when he refers to his icy hardness, and, climactically, to let drop the term "idealist." Such judgments, such epithets, are far too facile, commonplace. They are much too flattering, too much the sort of thing that the subject would find agreeable to his own peculiar variety of discontent; that is, a way of authenticating this discontent by turning it formally into a cold, "metallic," impenetrable mystery.

Burke's words, it must be recalled, were published in 1931. This is 1947, the year of *Monsieur Verdoux,* a statement of discontent, however personally or impersonally read, by far the most forthright Chaplin ever made. This movie is the explanation not so much of Chaplin's contradictions as of their dialectic consequence. To some extent (even Chaplin would agree), the mystery has now been penetrated and is even "colder" than the comedian himself could have thought it at the time of *City Lights*. For it was a "growing" mystery, an organic thing; in brief, a man's life. The whole story, Chaplin has recently said, has still not been told. He has yet, to quote him verbatim from a newspaper account, "to spill the beans." But at least he has spilled the beans with the power and knowledge at his command, as he managed to discover them. He has always worked hard, moreover, to evolve as a more and more conscious artist. One does not need inside information to know this fact; it has been patent on the surface. The majestic thing, the thing that reigns pre-eminent even above the clown's great diadem, is the fact that the universal mime, Charlie, is *not* the heart of the "metallic" mystery. For this mime was (he is now deceased) all heat, and invariably heat. It was the world that was cold.

**3** The simple, significant acts of Chaplin's life came before all generalizations and rationalizations of these acts, before the mature style of the successful actor, and even before the official birth of the sovereign Tramp. So it is better to follow the naïve, truth-tracing steps of Miss von Ulm as we go along the upward path of Chaplin's career.

For example, it was in London in 1905, when Chaplin was supposedly fourteen, that he enacted the role of Billy, a page boy, with William Gillette, in *The Painful Predicament of Sherlock Holmes.* Miss von Ulm describes the role as that of "a crafty young rascal who understands his master perfectly and accords him a sort of critical devotion." Perhaps this relationship could be transposed without much injury to the beginning of Charlie's relationship with his own father. There seems pertinent ground for this assumption in an incident related by Miss von Ulm, said to have occurred a year before Chaplin's appearance with Gillette.

Behind the scenes, Charlie happened to run into Sir Arthur Conan Doyle, whose manifest interest in the clever young performer stimulated a lively response in Chaplin. Without delay, the youngster proposed to Sir Arthur that they make an agreement to halve their mutual incomes for the rest of their lives. The remarkable thing here, at first sight, is the element of a *pact*—a fifty-fifty pact—made with an older man, obviously a symbolic echo of the paternal nourisher. Charlie no doubt sensed his own genius, but this intuition was not exactly equivalent to knowing its future worldly efficacy. The forlorn anxiety of the aristocratic infant that remained with him, the seizure of fear at the idea of economic responsibility—these early, insistent feelings propelled him into this childishly precocious proposal to the older man. . . .

I hardly pause here—as hardly elsewhere—to consider if this incident be a "true" one. It is enough that it is consistent both with a *profound* and *my* conception of Chaplin. This conception

has for one of its premises the hypothesis of the
unconscious as it exists in all of us; therefore, it is
possible to detect in the above-mentioned incident
a shadow of the impulse to bargain with the father
for an equal share in the mother. . . . Like many
an occurrence one might invent for a man's life, if
it did not happen it should have—and, indeed, it
might as well have. As we shall see later, it provides a curious echo for one of Charlie's late film
masterpieces, the very *City Lights* which he carried back to London with him as a trophy of
success.

**4** Two things now en-
tered the youthful Charlie's life with virtual simul-
taneity: the negative value of pantomime—its
silence, or absence of speech—and the negative
value of love, equally an "absence of speech." Miss
von Ulm reports that, as traveling vaudeville artists, Charlie and his company met with a severe
test in the Channel Islands, where the natives
spoke nothing but a French-English patois and the
audience greeted the sketch's funniest verbal sal-

lies with embarrassed silence. It was Charlie's ingenuity that came to the rescue; he understood the difficulty and promptly invented pantomime to substitute for the dropped dialogue; this did the trick. Later, Charlie became a member of Fred Karno's traveling troupe, significantly called "The Mumming Birds." We can only welcome, accordingly, the symmetry of the report that when, on tour, Charlie felt his first serious romantic pangs for a fair lady (a member of "the chorus"), he found himself . . . "speechless."

Without presuming to explain the situation, Miss von Ulm weaves a conventional, drawn-out romance of frustration between Charlie and this same young lady, whose name is given as Hetty. The account reads very much like a synopsis for one of Charlie's precarious screen romances, and even more impressive is the resemblance between an encounter with Hetty in a limousine, after years of separation, and the re-encounter of Monsieur Verdoux with a pretty waif, long after the foppish little murderer has spared her life; like Hetty, she is found the second time in the lap of luxury. The point is that Miss von Ulm's biography was published in 1940, long before Chaplin announced

**60**

anything about *Monsieur Verdoux*. The necessary implication is that such a biographical representation has self-evident value as a significant fiction, whether its source for Chaplin be real or imaginary. Of course, Chaplin himself attests to the factuality of his "first romance," as he does to that of other accounts given by Miss von Ulm, in his own book, *My Trip Abroad* (1921). Indeed, there his touch is so light and sentimental as to make the past seem (as it must have been somewhat) like a dream.

Such a correlation is like the reciprocal roles of fiction and truth in a Pirandellian comedy. Did the romantic, anticlimactic "limousine incident" *ever really occur* or was it *purely imaginary*? In the end, what difference does it make? My thesis is that the legend of the Tramp (with his inverted apotheosis as "Monsieur Verdoux") is compact and integral, and that this is the "biographical truth" of Chaplin's career. If there is any other truth, it is, perforce, peripheral or rates only the shallow grandeur of statistics.

**5** Yet surely we cannot ignore the words that fall from the hero's mouth, even if these—considering the high, mute style of the public comedian—are, so to speak (and however authentic), "unofficial." In 1915, the Chicago *Herald* reported these words of the little actor who had pushed his way up in Hollywood and rapidly become the rage of the time: "I dreamed," the hero said, "that I was the great romantic actor of the age—the ideal Romeo of the Photo-Shake-spearian." He was speaking of his first ambitions on arriving in Hollywood a few years before.

But can it be that he really believed then that he would enact dramatic roles? In view of the fact that it had been his routine as the dress-suited drunk, annoying music-hall performers from a box, that had attracted the original Hollywood offer, and in which he had toured the United States for three years, it seems almost impossible that he still retained whatever pristine dreams he may have had in England; possibly, however, he speculated that he would become rich with his magic pantomime and then . . . reveal himself as a "word man," a pronouncer of Shakespeare. Lewis Jacobs, in his book, *The Rise of the American Film,* ascribes to Chaplin an original desire, not only to be rich, but to be a "famed musician" and occupy "a seat in Parliament." But then, perhaps even now, little boys still want (or at least their parents want them) to become President of the United States. Such ambitions serve only, in the later life of the glorified success-man, to set off (as though he had wanted to be a street-car conductor or a fireman) the kind of ambition at which he did succeed. It is like saying that what has been achieved is in the same class as being a member of Parliament—*or better.* It is, too, a kind of boast.

The principal point is that the *goal* or *ideal* should be something distinct from the given occupation. There is a professional wiliness in all this as much as anything else. It is dramatic that someone at the top should confess he is, despite all, a "little man" like those of the multitude, "little" in comparison with the greatness of his aims. What Thomas Burke says to describe Chaplin's elusiveness and sadness, if circumscribed in meaning, could apply merely to that "glamour" which press agents strive to create about their employers. Yet

no question exists that in Chaplin's case the isolation and the private frustration are genuine. I
should say, however, that Chaplin often misnames
the content of these feelings, and their sources;
*conventionalizes* them not only as a sort of protective coloration, but also out of the fact that at certain stages of life (when very young, particularly)
we misconstrue our own feelings and wrongly
identify their subject matter.

To play Romeo: a legitimate ambition for an
actor, surely, and just as legitimate as an expression of puppy love. To speak, where he had not
spoken before: was *this* his crucial aim? But when
he saw the Hetty of the love legend he was struck
dumb, as one says, "with admiration." The cat of
some bygone day had taken his tongue. Now such
moments of embarrassed, surcharged silence are
not uncommon and not necessarily habitual. But
suppose there were a reason for their curious logic
and survival in the case of Charlie and his puppy-
love?

Need I say that children—all children—first sig-
nify what they want by inarticulate sound, inarticulate gesture? But well-bred children are trained
to speak "only when spoken to" or only when they

can express what they want in words. In such a manner, indeed, children are taught how to speak: by withholding something until it can be named. I suggest, from the grounds of common sense, that the source of the little comedian's pantomime is the wordlessness of a *taboo*. Something verbally forbidden, or on the contrary, a punishment for something too boldly named—these ghostly hypotheses survive in Charlie's historic pantomime. Take his famous original act of the drunk annoying the music hall performers with his stage-box antics. There is a period in which the child is strictly the audience, the parents strictly the performers. Is Chaplin's professional act not a perfect paradigm for an *ill-timed* demonstration in the presence of preoccupied parents? And the dress suit, used again and again in Chaplin's movies, is the aristocratic uniform. . . .

But here is the vital nexus: When sound pictures came, Chaplin's art received a very personal challenge. After all, the movies as a medium of pantomime offered him the perfection of his craft. Later on, as Chaplin's pictures became his own productions, subtitles, or *written speech*, began to carry the moral thoughts which he wished to in-

**65**

clude in the pictorial perspective—with which, specifically, he underlined the general, or "social," content of the tramp's adventures. For ten years Chaplin held out against talking pictures—when he did fully talk, first in *The Great Dictator* and then in *Monsieur Verdoux,* he said plenty, and it was murderous. Specter of the taboo—and of hate! . . . Finally, in this epos, we must reach the equation: *speech-hate*.

Meanwhile, however, Chaplin did all in his power to preserve the sanctity of pantomime, which was its *practical* silence; in fact, its virtual silence. It was not merely that, as in all serious films, for example, the lips moved, words were actually spoken but remained unheard, but that in the beginning Charlie's lips were sealed, he was literally mute; everything was conveyed in gesture and facial expression. This meant a unification of what in film is called "the silent medium": an *esthetic* unification. Chaplin rightly (as even D. W. Griffith) strove to reduce the necessity of subtitles. In *City Lights,* Chaplin not only wrote his own musical score, as though at least to keep the modified medium *personal,* but expressed personal sounds other than words, such as hiccoughing,

*triumph*

artificially, as, when he swallows a whistle, his hiccoughs are heard as "music." So the actual voice,
vehicle of words, remained truly taboo.

**6** If we think of the
young Chaplin, faced originally with the vista of
personal success in Hollywood, we can see him
visualize himself in Romeo's tights and jerkin,
wooing Juliet-Hetty perhaps, not only in sublime
pantomime, but also in words, albeit *unheard
words;* however beautiful, authentic: *unheard*—at
least by the audience. A cinematic veil of silence
is thus drawn across words even in the ideal, the
serious, dimension of art . . . in what, with inadvertent but startling fantasy, Charlie himself
termed "the Photo-Shakespearian." Yes, the "ideal"
sealed against sound: the sound-proofed studio of
the romantic, ideal moment!

When, in *Shoulder Arms,* Charlie wants to identify himself as an American to the French girl, he
has to resort to pantomime because of the lan-
guage barrier, so he "pantomimes" the stars and

**67**

stripes of the flag. This is superb comedy. But notice that it is quite artificial: there were probably
three or four easier ways for him to have let her
know he was American. The device has a curious
significance in the present perspective. In the
socio-sexual relations, there are dumb shows of
intention of a much more specific, if taboo'd,
nature.

**7** But in Hollywood, at
first, Charlie was doomed to be a pantaloon; to
echo, in effect, the music hall tradition of slapstick
and rowdiness. This, even after he succeeded in
the struggle to act in his own style. To make people laugh while undergoing suffering. Not to make
romantic love.

As I said, it is not that Chaplin expected to make
such love; he was fibbing to the interviewer, in a
way, by referring to a dream as though it were a
practical ambition or expectation. The interviewer
could not know that, in young Charlie's heart, the
medium of the film had materialized for him the
abstract dimension of dream: a dream of happi-

ness. The world of the perfect gesture. Ideally (and through artifice), this was the gesture of courtship, of the sexual wooing—sufficient unto itself, complete in its *being* rather than its *result*. In reality—that is, in extensible duration—it was something like the manner in which the Japanese tragedian died in a pantomime once enacted privately by Chaplin for Thomas Burke and the late Ralph Barton, related by Burke in the essay referred to above:

"I'll show you." Chaplin speaking. "He comes to his friend's house, and his friend hides him in a chest. The enemy search for him. They see the chest. The friend proves to them that it's locked, and assures them that it's empty. To make certain, two of them drive their swords through it. The swords come out clean. They're satisfied that the chest is empty, and go off. Then the friend opens the chest, and the man hiding comes out. He's dying. The swords went right through him, but as they were drawn out, he wrapped his robe round them and wiped them clean of blood. He was killed, but he couldn't let the enemy have the satisfaction of knowing they'd killed him. So he did that. And then died on the stage—upwards, in the most bew-tiful movements you could see."

As Chaplin spoke, he acted out all the parts. The death strokes occur in a tension of life-and-death silence. Then death is shown in the grandeur, the wordless grandeur, of the very last seconds of life. Perhaps Chaplin conceived the death of his dream in the same way, silently wiping off the "articulate" blood so that the enemy should not know—"the enemy"; who should this be, in terms transferring this actual death drama to the drama of the love-dream's death, but the *loved one herself*?—the woman whose words "killed"?

**8** How should one presume to call this man Chaplin a clown? Well, who is it who laughs at a child's woe but an adult, specifically perhaps the parent?—at, I should say, the child's silent, speechless, woe? The tragedy is thus his inner suffering, as it is Canio's inner suffering that he should evoke the laughter of the audience while more than a mere dumb show is going on, while his heart is beating in such excruciating articulacy. The prototype here, as applied to Charlie, is not the cuckolded husband, but the child himself, whose suffering becomes a variety of clowning for the parent, the adult spectator. As soon as the attention of the preoccupied parent is secured, he (or she) laughs rather than sympathizes. In the same way, puppy-love is not taken seriously, and for adults, especially the parents, is often matter for amusement.

But if we remind ourselves of the present perspective, created in the two previous sections of this study, if we think of Charlie, the immortal Charlie, as the child aristocrat, the person with a dream of victory in his little fists, and with of course the erotic dream entrancing everything, over all, as it must ever be with us—then we can *laugh* only as we used to in the theater when we saw Charlie's antics of frustration; his grace in clumsiness; his articulacy in inarticulacy. But we cannot laugh now. It is not merely that, thus, we perceive Charlie's "pathetic" moments; the moments that Lewis Jacobs, for example, has called agonizing, when Charlie stands stripped of love and the world at the end of one of his comedies. It is that we see in every dynamic gesture the

**71**

*clowning* of one who is but parodying the serious; of one who is making a complex substitution: of *action* for contemplation, of *action* for words, of irrelevant action for relevant action.

Chaplin is, of course, a poet. Isn't the poet's first act a *dream of action*? It is action, essentially, musicalized; action whose meaning is converted into a speech mirroring its perfection of harmony, which is primarily an inner perfection; it is the "aristocratic" presumption of the "absolute" dreamer. The literal acting-out, then, becomes a kind of vulgarization; a needless display in the physical world, however exquisitely stylized. "In the beginning was the Word." This is the law and the lyric of its perfection, not the enactment of the law and the drama of its imperfection. And what was the word for the baby Charlie? What for any baby but the pure symbol of the world objectified? The sign of a *relation*. The working out of the verbal in Charlie's infantile life may well have had something definitely frustrating in it—some kind of experience threw him back on the pure pantomime, on the wordless gesture, as a sacrosanct realm, the *desirable* sign for the worldly relation. What does it really matter what it was, literally, precisely, in our hero's life? A dream at the mother's breast, broken into by the father's word, the father's voice . . . the wordless pantomime of the parents' gestures which the child wished to interrupt. . . . Yes, associated with pantomime as a profession, Charlie's dream of happiness, essentially wordless, could have been connected perfectly logically with an essentially wordless action of life.

The genius of gesture in Chaplin—this becomes nothing but the faculty of acting out the fate of this dream; it is the galvanizing of the dream into objective, physical gestures: wordless because without—shall I say?—*verbal consent*. Usually, physical union—every kind of "contract"—is first signified as verbal or written consent: *words*. The essence of consent resides in token rather than in deed; in formal promises of fulfillment however casual, laconic.

The passionate wooer not only may get on his knees and implore; if desperate, ingenious, and precipitate—short of violence—he may virtually act out the love gestures in a kind of pantomime, flexibly symbolic. Are the stars and stripes of Doughboy Charlie's pantomime to the French girl not also substantive for *a bed*? . . . What would

**73**

the *star* alone be, what the straight-shooting *stripe*? So, in the subjective dream of happiness, the lyrical moment, all takes place in the dumb show of poetry, the inner realm of absolute harmony, where the "word" is the pure dream of action.

It is this fact which Charlie conveyed so faultlessly, with such masterfully economic genius, to audiences that included even savages. It is a happiness that overflows with an inner sweetness; as artless, in its dynamic, spontaneous surface as the flirt of a bird's wing, the high back-kick of a rabbit. It is the timeless and spaceless freedom of the happy child-in-love. How poignant, sometimes, was Charlie's look of incredulous surprise at the world's tasteless interruption. The fortunes of the tramp Charlie, no matter what his incidental role— a reformed derelict or a preacher, a count or an unemployed laborer—were only the logical result of stubborn clinging to the inner sanctity of this highly irrational dream; a trance of happiness expressed in the endless repertory of Charlie's precious gestures. The "French" kick—indeed a sort of rabbit kick—which he borrowed from Max Linder's similar burlesque of a dandy, and made indelibly his; the monumentally fragile shrug; the deft, lightning-like adjustment of the derby; the cannily cosmic, single revolution of the cane; the gyration of the mustache that seemed to tickle his nose like some transcendent odor—all these things were child-aristocratic mannerisms, a heraldic defiance of the worst that reality could do, or not do.

Charlie "the tramp philosopher" carried around with him the word unspoken, the perfect word, of love. His figure is a degeneration of sartorial style and of romantic (literal) stature, and so "clownish," but in ratio as there is a diminution, a deterioration, in the physical world, there is a "heroicalizing," an aggrandizement, in the spiritual world; or rather, there *was* in the young, the infantile, perspective of the artist. Silent pantomime for many years in Charlie's artistic-professional life stood for the absolute, the perfect happiness, as opposed to reality; in this paradise, seen again and again (especially in the dream cottage in *Modern Times*), the consent of both wooed and wooer is wordless because all is automatic, all is timeless and spaceless, in the dream within the existential dream-of-art.

All dreams are tall.

And you—even you, child aristocrat—had to work for your dreams. And with the flaw weighing you down.

**9** Height speaks for itself. Before Hetty, tallness would have spoken for Charlie. Since it was not there, he could not speak. Words would have done no good—no practical good. So the virtually mute mimicry of life dragged on. Even spoken, as of course they were, words could do no good. So this *symbolic silence,* in the dimension of reality, became distance, physical separation from Hetty.

The distance between dream and action. The distance between word and deed. The distance between camera and actor. The distance between screen and spectator. The distance between love and hate. All these became somehow one, indivisible illusion, so that Chaplin himself said: "Comedy is life viewed from a distance." But an even truer motto of the clown's triumph, I would say, is:

"Distance is full of silence."

# IV
### *the gestures in front of and behind the screen*

**one** The thing that most impressed the Hollywood comedy world, when Chaplin first arrived there and met hostility and skepticism, was his *falling technique*. . . . To fall precisely, gracefully, with supreme finality . . . perhaps this is possible only when a dream is also collapsing. But more than one phase (as the falling-artist knows) comprises the process of a fall. In our American way, I might remark that Charlie the youth fell first when he fell for Hetty, and he

77

has thus, in a sense, never stopped falling. All along, he has been *practicing* . . . for the "true" fall, for utter submission to the Fatal Woman he would actually meet in life.

It is the clown who takes a tumble. As the category of the comedian rises in dignity, the tumble becomes the more figurative; always, in this respect, the clown is repeating his original fall from human grace. This conception, of course, has an even more serious connotation: Lucifer, the dark angel, fell from heavenly grace, became God's enemy. And the two, Adam and Eve, made of the Fall a legend with a capital letter. Remove the white grease paint, and we find in the comic mime a suffering lover—invariably the grotesque mask hides real grief, profound grief, camouflaged by the gay, frivolous surface. A figure so *simple* as Charlie the Tramp, and so supreme at the same time, must secrete in its tissues all legendary sinners: the black-browed, and the cheeks white with innocence. Of Lucifer and his epic speech, we will hear anon. Now it is the old Adam in the young Charlie to whom we bear witness.

**2** In his essay, Thomas Burke remarks how often he could tell Chaplin was reliving the past as he made his films: "When I saw *The Kid* and its implied attitude to orphanages," he observes, "I knew where that bit came from. And the incident in *Shoulder Arms,* when all but himself receive a parcel, and the instructions on table manners in *The Kid,* how to eat with the back of a knife—I knew where that came from." Surely all this has basic truth, and although Burke does not go into the romantic incidents of sex in Chaplin's films, the same sort of parallel would hold with regard to the actual love odyssey of the comedian, on one hand, and the romances he invented for the screen, on the other. Here, however, the matter is, inevitably, more speculative, metaphorical. Just as Chaplin received so rich a pleasure in going back to the very dining room in which he had eaten in the London orphanage, thus recapturing (as he said) a "skin" he had once "shed," still with his "odor about it," so he must have drawn on his experiences for innumerable other little effects, and so achieved something of

**79**

the revivification of lost times that Proust did. But Chaplin—insofar as the objectivity of his screen art goes—can by no means be compared with Proust as perfecter of self through art.

As we run the parallel lines of life and art in Chaplin's life, we have to bear in mind that he was not perpetually in a state of tranquillity, not in a quiescent condition of "total recall," but that life kept pace with his art; that, in the manner of the romantic, art and life were somehow ever confused; and far from conquering "reality" (as Proust conquered his environment and his intimate physical being, bending all their pain and narrowness to the liberating paean of his art), Chaplin remained one who perpetually escaped into art to achieve the perfection of gesture he saw in Japanese tragedy. The Little Tramp was definitely an underdog, and Chaplin could triumph over the Tramp's environment only symbolically, insofar as gradually, in the over-all view, his professional success enabled him entirely to control his own productions. He could do as he pleased on and off screen—at least theoretically. There must be a material distinction, however, between Chaplin's *artistic* success and his *professional* success;

the former's result did not always coincide with the triumph of the latter. This inequality in Chaplin's life is shown in a myriad of ways.

**3** We are now face to face with the all-crucial problem of *the actor,* so central to Chaplin's *epos.* As Charlie, he was the fictitious character who, like Canio, played a part on the stage and inevitably had to submit to another dimension as well—that of reality; a reality reflecting his make-believe, and tragic because what was artistic pretense, turned inside out, became bitter reality.

Ah, but the legend of Charlie the Little Tramp is not the Pagliacci legend! No, it is not so simple. The true split in the duration of existence is hidden; it is never an obvious dualism: a question of the theater and "life," art and reality; it is never altogether visible on the surface because it is too deep in the protagonist. The "stage," the fictitious dimension in regard to Charlie, is *his own person—* the little man, the child aristocrat, the flawed

**81**

jester; on this metaphoric stage of self, the tramp *opposes* the aristocrat, the child *opposes* the man, the lover *opposes* the hater—in sum, the professional, the *success*-image, opposes the amateur, the *failure*-image. Whatever happens to this pathetic character, Charlie, it is "all reality," all a single dimension, just as, in the end, there is only (as Proust said) one life: this one. Chaplin has arisen to play the violin in the middle of the night. He has been so bored that he has stayed in bed two and three days at a time. These actions are pure phenomena of romantic disquiet and luxurious ennui. Yet they are inseparable from the romanticism and laziness of the Tramp, who, in one film, was a violinist.

The life of art, however, opens up the purely imaginative dimension: it serves not only to interpret and systematize life but to add to it. The approach of the poet to life is that of a master who wishes to grasp all its laws and render them, no matter in what medium; in this way, he recreates his own existence and the world's, and with the quantity of himself adds to the sum of reality, enlarges it.

What of Charlie? Chaplin became a poet

*manqué,* not a great comic mime whose art (like Deburau's) was to perfect the actor's instrument the way a dancer perfects his body, in order to make it do wondrous things, which provide only a showcase for its skill, but rather a great clown whose "act" is continuous: the never-ending and precarious dramatizing of what happens to such a mime when thrust into the realities of life itself. In tucking the toe of one great shoe under the door of Life and never removing it, but pursuing Charlie's fortunes in a pattern of time and space, Chaplin broke with the tradition of the clown represented by such as Grimaldi and the perennial Fratellini. It is "all one life" only summatively, asymmetrically, not essentially, symmetrically. The Pirandellian perspective of "fiction within fiction" (and correspondingly "reality within reality") exists amply, especially in the early slapstick comedies of Chaplin, where the "behind the scenes" motif recurs, specifically in the two-reeler of 1916, *Behind the Screen.* But, from the very first, Chaplin exploited the prototypic role of the stage-box drunk who disrupts the show, with the change that now Charlie is behind scenes as a property man; his function, however, remains that of disruption—the disruption of the "art fiction"; partly deliberate, but mostly inadvertent.

Chaplin has hidden the tramp's personality behind many disguises. Charlie, like David, always *aspired*—but he usually won success only (as in the 1914 two-reeler *His Prehistoric Past,* in which he is a caveman named Weakchin who overthrows the ruler) by dint of dreaming it all. He even played the successful lover—the character who overwhelms the party's most beautiful girl. But that was only once, long ago. He knew—and we knew—it was a useless maneuver, a charade; the real character was always the gentle derelict, the pathetic, golden, fantastic tramp, who for the moment impersonates, literally or in the art-life perspective, someone more solidly connected with society than he is.

Whether convict disguised as minister or tramp masquerading as Count, whether bona fide bourgeois on a holiday or honest laborer, Charlie is one whose only solid connection with reality is love; his irrepressible desire to express his admiration and tenderness for the opposite sex. This comes out in its clear imaginative form in *Sunnyside,* when Charlie, as the overworked lone factotum in a summer hotel, gets knocked into a ditch while riding a cow, and in his unconscious delirium imagines himself dancing with nymphs in flowered fields.

4 We cannot hide from the overt facts of Chaplin's private life, which have won front-page stories throughout his career. These very facts provide the triple dimension of the successful comedian's struggle with his alter ego, the Little Tramp.

What was the perfection of this creature of the artist Chaplin's? It was the sheer outward mechanics of a personality secreting a dream of happiness: a semimoronic dream (a fool's dream) which sat enthroned in the childlike man and resisted all onslaughts by the world. In London, 1921, when he first returned there in triumph, Chaplin amused one of his hosts and the guests by dancing à la Nijinski. On film and off, he was propelled into the dance gesture; on shipboard once, while touring Europe with May Reeves, he performed "the dance of the tissue." A photograph of the incident in Miss von Ulm's book reveals the "tissue" as, apparently, toilet paper; Chaplin's pantomimic genius, if nothing less, no doubt saved him from any rebukes.

But, on the screen, the dreaming tramp was like a dancing doll: mute and inert in a preternatural trance until prodded, "wound up," by the touch, coarse or delicate, of the world; then he is thrust into action and, because he is a "character doll," he does not precisely dance; instead, he pantomimes his bewilderment, his shyness, his trembling passion, his terror, his frantic efforts at equilibrium. A wonderful and exact instance of these same "frantic efforts" took place in *The Circus* when, as the tightrope-walking clown, Charlie has to keep his footing on the rope although a troop of monkeys are climbing all over him. The tightrope situation means precariousness: an exquisiteness of balance achieved while meeting opposition as well as encouragement; fancifully, the monkeys themselves may be construed as Charlie's own inept imitators, all eventually routed.

Across a certain distance the comedian was ever looking back at the tramp, as though de-

termined to rescue him from the pain of his predicament by emphasizing his beautiful spiritual
qualities, his almost "saintly" ability to sub-
limate. Before Charlie's curious bout with his
first official alter ego, the dipsomaniac capitalist
of *City Lights*, he played his first double role in
a two-reel film issued in 1921, *The Idle Class*,
made after his London visit and following the
social fetes given him on his return to New York.

As in more than one of Chaplin's films, the action devolves here on mistaken identity. Charlie
assumes the roles of a wealthy fop and his regular
dudish version of the little tramp. The latter falls
in love with the former's wife and daydreams his
life with her. Chased by the police, he blunders
into a masquerade ball, where the lady in question takes him for her husband in costume. Her
real husband, however, appears in a suit of armor,
from which he cannot extricate himself, even his
face being hidden. When he is finally freed and
the mistake discovered, the little tramp has to
make a quick exit.

I point to the suit of armor in which the rich
man is trapped. Is the occupant not Chaplin himself, the "genuine dandy" as opposed to the myth-

ical figure of the Little Tramp? And is not the armor a suitable symbol for that "mailed hood" to which I referred previously as a metaphor: the metaphor of Chaplin's professional crusade to win fame and money, and which he donned by his father's bier? In a sense, he is doomed to stay in this armor (to live the life of Charles Spencer Chaplin, comic artist), but, when freed of its onus, he witnesses the flight of his dream figure, the Little Tramp, into the cosmos beyond the film frame; formally, into nonexistence. Yet no gesture, surely, occurred *behind the scenes* of the tramp's adventures which was not somehow duplicated in front of them—in that continuous stream of invention which Chaplin increasingly lavished on his character creation.

**5** Indeed, Chaplin spent more money on creating the elaborate saga of Charlie than he did on his wives and other women, or than he did on the actresses whom opinion has it that he loved to consider mere un-

shaped clay for his sculptor's hand. It is true that
none of Chaplin's leading ladies has ever made
a name independently of his tutelage excepting
one, Paulette Goddard; Mildred Harris won a
transient acting fame principally as Mildred
Harris Chaplin, his ex-wife. These leading ladies,
doubtless chosen for qualities consistent with
images met in private daydreams, form a proces-
sion parallel with the march of Chaplin's marriages and enthusiasms.

A strikingly prophetic incident is innocently
related by Miss von Ulm to show the brooding,
yet quite undisguised, frustration which Chaplin
could feel in the presence of some beautiful, unattainable woman. He had already found acclaim
abroad when, back in Hollywood, he went to a
restaurant with two ladies (one supposedly his
"latest") and recognized a member of the French
embassy whom he had met. With this gentleman
was a tall, lovely, aristocratic blonde, the "Baronesse T———." Without touching his food and
hardly heeding his companions, Chaplin fixed on
the Baronesse a continual stare, transparently one
of deep desire. Everything he was feeling was
transmitted through simple facial expression and

complete silence. Relentlessly he pursued his behavior to everyone's uneasiness and the ruin of
the evening.

The incident, which occurred about 1925, apparently had no consequences. But several years
later, Chaplin happened to meet another tall,
beautiful blonde, Virginia Cherrill by name, and,
while of little talent, she was engaged as his
leading lady for *City Lights*. Although her sudden
fame went to her head, and she was hard to
handle largely because she arrived at the studio
late and worn out, Chaplin managed to hammer
her into the shape he wanted.

It is not only that this episode suggests a
character-mechanism; i.e., Chaplin's hypothetical
practice of substituting a real "leading lady" for
some object of unrealized desire (here the
Baronesse T———); much more than this is
present—and aptly in the form of artistic invention. When Charlie, in *City Lights*, first encounters the blind flower seller (Miss Cherrill),
she mistakes him for a wealthy gentleman and
offers him a flower. Thus, again the theme of
mistaken identity, now with special significance.
For the girl is *blind,* and this permits the coinci-

dence of offering the flower, intrinsically a symbol of herself.

Blindness is a *flaw*. And it is equivalent to the silence which, in the light of this analysis, cannot be taken as other than the token at once of Charlie's dream of happiness and its automatic frustration. Automatically, the dream is given— but by indirection, as a result of a flaw in the one opposite, *the woman.*

( . . . *Indirection*. As sound developed in Chaplin's films, we have to note that voices first appeared indirectly; that is, by radio or television, as in the factory of *Modern Times*. . . .)

If the flower seller is blind, she cannot tell anything about Charlie's looks; for example, that he is short; so momentarily the tramp is received into his own dream in the imagination of the flower girl and lives there in timeless bliss. But reality is also present. The girl is one who inadvertently, by defection, "kills" with a kind of silence, a veil of unawareness. And Charlie, à la "Japanese hero" wishes to "die" without his "enemy" knowing it; he does not, therefore, although in acute torture himself, let her know he is not tall, elegant, and handsome: he wishes to

**91**

exist in her transcendent illusion, but of course
he cannot. Everything Charlie was as an artist
depended upon *vision*; blindness completely
negated him and left the world open for pure
imagining. In such a manner as this film incident
provided, Charlie's flaw met its mathematical
reciprocity in "reality."


**6** But this movie, like
life, went on; moreover, in the texture of
actuality, in the complicated dialectic of living,
the "throwback" is always turning up; the *throwback*: i.e., what has been incompletely, incorrectly
assimilated. While Chaplin was undergoing the
difficult drama of finding his leading ladies to fit
the roles of his imagination, he was having real-
life romances just as difficult in which the Fool's
master was a great ladies' man: a veritable heart-
breaker and—if certain observers are to be believed—a Don Juan. But should we say that
Chaplin (or indeed Charlie himself) was "Don
Juan with a telescope"?

Once Charlie, during one of his habitual wanderings through the city, discovered in New York a huge telescope which he ordered Kono, his Japanese secretary, to buy for him. Finally, the unwieldy object, to Kono's dismay, was installed on the terrace of Chaplin's Hollywood home, where according to Miss von Ulm it commanded a view of John Barrymore's home, unknown (presumably) to that gentleman. This same John Barrymore was a famous lover in real life and indeed even filled the role of Don Juan for the movies. One recalls Chaplin's aphorism already given: "Comedy is life viewed from a distance. . . ."

The telescope would be a transposed symbol of height—the elongated etherealization and sublimation of the *flaw*.

**7** If comedy is the result of distance, then tragedy, inversely, would be the result of propinquity, and, as applied to the sexual field, tragedy would be tangible, immediate, unspeaking sex; a reality too close to bear, hence the distance . . . "tragedy," Chaplin concluded his aphorism, "life in a close-up."

An abundance of evidence exists pointing to Chaplin's taste for small, dark girls, preferably very young. Girls, that is to say, about as tall as he; thus "short" or "tall," probably, according to the end of the emotional telescope through which Chaplin's mood bade him look at them. His first wife, Mildred Harris, though petite and only fifteen when he first met her, was fair, yet his second wife, Lita Grey, was (being part Mexican) dark and small as well as young. These two marriages, especially the second, were apparently Chaplin's bitterest experiences, and part of the bitterness must have arisen from the fact that most of the trouble of the second was his neglected wife's demand for an alimony he considered excessive; the result was that the whole thing was fought in court, Chaplin was royally smeared by the press, and his bright fame considerably tarnished. Thus the Little Tramp's position, from that of being a cherished idol of the people, threatened to become that of a heartless, selfish, and even vicious specimen of manhood, unworthy of being husband or father.

Neither of these first marriages, according to most of the symptoms, was idealistic, the second less nearly so than the first. Apparently, in a quite ordinary way, Chaplin grew bored with his wife and sought companionship elsewhere. Reputedly, Pola Negri and another Hollywood actress, shielded as "Maisie" by Miss von Ulm, were among his intimate friends; the former's reign, during an official engagement, was tempestuous and rather brief; his interest in the latter continued pretty steadily through the years, went through his marriage with Lita Grey, and—at least so far as printed publicity went—had an unmarred clandestine status.

Popular legend has it that a number of women, including Pola Negri, "threw themselves at" Chaplin; the most distracted, we might note, waylaid him and tried to break into his house. It is odd that while similar things must have happened to other prominent actors, there are very few histories of this kind comparable to Chaplin's, and none at all that have spanned so many years and become identical with their hero's character. Searching for an explanation, one may sift the inevitable conditions to uncover the hypothesis that perhaps it was just when public scandal threatened that Chaplin became most determined to be adamant and revengeful toward a persistent woman with whom he was through. And perhaps this mood obtained in proportion to his fool-hardiness in having become involved with certain women and his ineptitude in handling the affairs.

I think one may experimentally indicate a certain sexual temper in Chaplin the diurnal man; a temper impulsive, negligent, even with a malicious element in it. Why did he never marry Pola Negri—or "Maisie"? It seems likely that Chaplin was always tempted to marry, but that—even when he could have done so—he feared to become bound to anyone who might prove a match for him in temperament, will, and self-reliance.

Condescension, when it is not built on the securest of power, is a risky factor. Sexual condescension, founded on compensated inferiority, would be very dangerous. Chaplin's strictly off-stage behavior must have become ordinary subject matter for gossip so that it, too, became part of his "legend." After all, his very practice of making "finds" among the would-be actresses that thronged the gates of Hollywood studios was an advertisement to girls who had heard of his extreme susceptibility to feminine charms. Chaplin, more or less deliberately, must certainly have counted on this double-edged aspect of his reputation to act both ways, to help him find the right actresses and the right companions. That some women must have earned both positions at once seems only plausible. And that, according to the ambivalence of the character pattern being analyzed here, they must have shuttled precariously in Chaplin's mind between these two positions, seems equally plausible.

**8** And yet I pause to ask: Did Chaplin guarantee his "ideal woman," who might be termed The Actress in his life, by relegating her to the romantic distance where, for example, Don Quixote situated Dulcinea?—beyond the possible sphere of marriage, that is to say, where she would be in relation to him only as a woman of clay would be to the sculptor as he molded her, or as an actress to her director? This is the Trilby-Svengali relationship that has also become part of Chaplin's legend.

Edna Purviance was Chaplin's leading lady for fifteen years, having come to Hollywood like any other girl anxious to break in; no other actress has been with him nearly so long. A lush blonde, and about as tall as Chaplin, she was very ductile material but far from a brilliant actress. It is suggestive to recall that Trilby was not only tall and blonde (like Baronesse T———) but that she had no art when not under her master's spell. Especially because of the simplified, mathematically arranged action of Chaplin's films, his leading ladies tended to seem "soulless" foils, mere obliging mechanisms; we cannot fail to associate their behavior with erotic passivity. Edna Purviance, Miss von Ulm claims, worshiped Chaplin as virtually her creator and was a perfect subject for his manipulation. Did he or did he not love her? Maybe he did not dare permit himself to. Maybe, whether he did or not, it was against the rules of his own subjective myth.

An important discrepancy, a special exemptive condition, must be considered in respect to

Chaplin as Don Quixote and Svengali; a condition
that dialectically transcends while it disqualifies.
He himself, as the Little Tramp, is part of the
spell and remains, nevertheless, creator of the
spell; he is not only consciously its hero, but
consciously its director, its stage-manager. Chaplin, when under the spell of an emotion, is
Charlie, the little tramp, having his dream of
happiness; the dissolution of this dream-spell occurs when reality intervenes, when the spell is
tested by duration in objective, worldly action.
So the Ideal Woman is but *part of* the Ideal
Element; when she is pure distance, the spirit of
a silent, inert idyl, she is safe, perfected (like a
painting or a sculpture). Such, inverted in
Charlie's direction, is the incident of the blind
flower seller, in whose imagination Charlie is
momentarily painted as a handsome wealthy
gentleman. But when the woman becomes "tangible," available in the flesh, her fatal limitation is
revealed; it is when she is related to the Little
Tramp, vehicle of the ideal—when she becomes
Galatea *vivante*—that her tangible quality shows
itself, and when Charlie is later actually seen by
the flower seller, her sight recovered through his

beneficence, *his* tangible quality shows. *Touch and spoil* . . . or *see and spoil*. It is the same.

In this respect there is a meaningful anecdote told by Clare Sheridan, who was a sculptress, and six inches taller than Chaplin, in her autobiography, *The Naked Truth*. She and Chaplin, accompanied by her little son, a chauffeur, a chef, and Kono, tried to escape civilization by going on a camping trip. The pair succeeded to the extent of spending some intensely idyllic and tender moments alone by the campfire in the evening. The firelight, playing on the comedian's rumpled curls, seems to have given him an elfin charm. The sculptress was eager to do him in clay, and she eventually completed a bust which Chaplin had cast in bronze. The trip was finally spoiled by public curiosity and, as usual, reporters. Stripped of his motley and throwing himself into the carefree life of the outdoors, delicate-boned Charlie must have seemed a kind of diminutive Pan, a male Galatea in a sweater . . . Yet that the female Pygmalion, an Amazon compared with Charlie, must have neglected to visualize the legendary dénouement to the implicit situation is humorously hinted by a letter included in her

**100**

autobiography: "Dear Charlie, How funny it would have been if . . . And on the whole not so unsuitable but . . . "

(Dots in the original published version.)

**9** "Distance is full of silence." It is propinquity, the physical principle, that "speaks for itself"—does not, alas, require words. When Cyrano de Bergerac, however, is induced by Christian to speak for him, Cyrano is a voice appearing in a physical mask of the ideal. Cyrano always mocks himself, plays the clown out of irony and bitterness: he has a flaw; soldier, poet, wit, only his prodigy of a nose prevents him from being the ideal cavalier. Physical beauty, like everything else, speaks for itself— or should. Because Christian could not woo Roxane, Cyrano had to do it for him. Cyrano makes the gesture behind the scene, Christian in front of it; voice is transposed with physique while only one man is mentally visible to Roxane. So only "one man" is visible to the women in

Chaplin's life whether on the stage with him or off it with him. This is why Charlie's costume is itself a suit of armor imprisoning a tall dream.

**10** Suppose we assume a hidden Narcissist in Chaplin the artist-worker. Charlie is the fictional being who dreams of being Charles Spencer Chaplin before whom a woman prostrates herself. If Don Quixote de la Mancha, the armored knight, idealizes a woman, it is the world he fights in her honor; she is not the opponent. But, in Chaplin's case, we must assume a shifting struggle between him and his idealized dream of woman. In this light, we can understand how Chaplin shunned, as much as wanted, the typical female specter of his life: the one who ostensibly wanted to prostrate herself before him, because, in the realistic dimension, she might be after fame and comfort as much as after him. Chaplin, the inert ideal, is actively haunted by a tall-short, dark girl carrying an ambivalently passive, questionably sincere worship. When the comedian first met Paulette Goddard, whom he later married, she was blonde; when she let her natural hair, which was dark, grow in again, it must have been "reality" emerging ominously, if somehow welcome, from the golden ideal. But ambiguity was bound to attach itself to such inverse magic. After all, *in reality*, Quixote's own Dulcinea was only a milkmaid.

The real Chaplin's protection against "the dark lady" of the legend was Charlie's costume, a kind of armor. Behind this armor, Chaplin was an invisible wizard manipulating all imaginary creatures—and to some extent, and illusively, all real creatures coming under his spell. Chaplin's self-creation, the tramp, was one who narcissistically dreamed of being the perfection of Charles Spencer Chaplin, short man. This narcissistic self-conceit was perpetually being destroyed by reality, not only in the art dimension, the life of the tramp-adventurer, but in the real dimension, the life of the man who came to create *Modern Times, The Great Dictator,* and *Monsieur Verdoux* . . . the man who created his own myopic odyssey.

**11** If Chaplin dreamed up the Little Tramp by projecting him onto the screen of the imagination, this projected self in turn reflected the figure of the actor-director and real-life Don Juan; a successful, a powerful, man but not a perfect or a happy man. The Chaplinesque Cyrano was both in front of and behind the scene, for the comedy-drama took place not only on the stage but in life, including the stage. Charlie as clown physically "fronted" for Chaplin as man; in this way, "the flaw" was both physically and spiritually extroverted, displaced from its inner taboo . . . but not rendered, of course, in the romantic imagination of a Rostand. Chaplin's epos has nothing if not modern complexity.

The dual roles in the comedies, then, reflected the existence of an alter ego, typified by the myth-figure and the man. Thus all the various impersonations by Charlie (he even impersonated a woman) were but symbolic illustrations of alternation between the two poles of the ego and its other; a temporary impersonation of one of the two personalities (*man* and *actor*) by the other. If, as in *The Vagabond* (1916), he is the usual little tramp, here in love with a "gipsy girl" who turns out to be the kidnaped child of wealthy parents, he attempts to emulate the art of the painter with whom the girl falls in love; thus symbolizing the tramp's reflection of the artist Chaplin, whose great talent helps make him attractive to women. Suggestively, moreover, Charlie's violin has proven no match for the gipsy music, as his amateurish painting succumbs to the "true" painter's. In a romantic-ironic climax, the girl, carried away by her mother in an auto, suddenly understands that she really loves Charlie and has the car turn back to the place where she has left him standing forlorn. Here is an ideal pantomime of the woman who realizes that she loves Charlie the simple Adam rather than Chaplin the complex artist. And how has "Charlie" triumphed?—merely by *being himself*: a masculine image, however poor, untalented (the archetype of Christian in *Cyrano de Bergerac*).

**12** More than one writer has emphasized that Chaplin as a young man habitually aroused in women "the protective, mothering instinct." What beauty speaks for itself so much as that of a little boy in front of his mother, who but he needs begging words so little to supplement his silent image? So speech becomes token of a special talent, a conscious and purposive form of eloquence; such as it signified, indeed, for Cyrano as well as for Romeo, the great lover of the young Chaplin's dreams.

In the normal romantic conception, the poetic words of love are but formal extensions of feeling, conventions that decorate life and supplement the gestures of love. *But what if speech were split from gestures?* Then they would possess a separate genius. An imagined lack of the genius of words (perhaps as units of persuasion) might effect a complete displacement into the genius of gestures as units of persuasion; i.e., in the esthetic realm, as a variety of dance-ceremony. So any lack (or, positively speaking, any flaw) means compensation, exaggeration in another field. Yet

**106**

compensation, however automatic the mechanism's adjustment, requires constant replenishment, application; in brief, it means *work*.

When Charlie pantomimed for his mother, who was short and dark, he was not a mere inert image pleasing her, nor could this "dance" have been a *direct* method of wooing her. No; rather it was, especially in its cultivation as a profession for the boy of five, a form of work: a genius put to the grindstone. What might have been a weapon of the incestuous motive was a weapon of implicit livelihood—its prospect pictured (at such an age) in terms of work rather than pleasure. Indeed, art—however transcendent in its poetry—could not be deprived by young Charlie of its element of labor. Pantomime, for him, became work as much as esthetic indulgence; only natural, then, the perpetual fusion of the work gesture and the dance gesture in his comic pantomime.

In many short films, in which Charlie assumes a variety of crafts and jobs, including the climactic *Modern Times*, where he is a factory hand, the movements of work are invariably rhythmicalized, burlesqued, and finally explode into anarchy while still operative. Work is thus sublimated into

**107**

dance, but at the expense of its practical nature, as though this sort of sublimation (art?) were all that made it tolerable. One thinks of one of Chaplin's aphorisms as concretely applicable here: "Art is the treatment applied to work and has nothing to do with subject-matter."

Of course, if he could have *told* his mother something, "spoken" . . . But, from the viewpoint of the little boy, she seemed so *tall*, unreachable.

**13** Charlie's pantomime before his leading ladies, his courtship—it was fascinating for him to plot the ways in which it could succeed ("work") and the ways in which it couldn't. The Unattainable (shall I say the tall, blonde, beautiful Unattainable?) was always present in Chaplin's myth because the result was never to be measured properly by its motive, its calculation. Alas, *work* can always be measured by its immediate motive: money. Charlie's art was always precise; whether merely funny, or pathetic and deeply touching, the spectacle of his pantomime had no logic of moral consequence: the heroine might or might not consent to marry him. This principle of Charlie's lack of control over the moral nature of his effect on a woman (*comic* here would apply to successful effect, *tragic* to frustrated effect) was illustrated pointedly on a symbolic level in *The Circus* when, as the clown performer, he is "funny when he doesn't intend to be and pathetic when he tries to be comic."

This ambivalence of effect could be beautiful and artistic when *in front of the scenes,* where it could be controlled, exactly equated with intention. But *behind the scenes,* where it could not be controlled, where it equivocated with the emotions of the powerful and practical Sancho Panza, who had confiscated the Don's poetic ideal—here, was this ambivalence not ominously ugly, ominously tragic?

# V
*coronation*
*of the*
*underdog*

**one** *The Kid* grew up.
Steadily, if unevenly, with many throwbacks.
There is a parallel between Chaplin's own life
and the famous film of this title which he made
with the then unknown Jackie Coogan as co-star.
Released in 1921, it was the most expensive and
ambitious as well as the most serious of the comedian's movies. Doubtless stirring in Chaplin was the
desire to approach and evaluate his past by a kind
of reconstruction, instead of dealing with it fitfully
and obliquely as he had in all his other films. Pov-

erty and erotic frustration, the great little dream, the disruption of order and work—all these had been present from the beginning of his film career, but not till now the logical, literal birth of the urchin: budlike Charlie of the Kennington slum.

The Moses or man-of-destiny myth is repeated in the beginning of *The Kid*, where a bastard child is left by its destitute mother (Edna Purviance) in a limousine; the limousine is stolen and the child tossed into an alley. Charlie finds him. Exactly the number of years pass (five) that occurred between Charlie's birth and his father's death, the moment when he realized his destiny as an artist. In the film, Charlie is the kid's foster father, his guardian angel, and the kid grows up a parody of the oddly austere tramp. Charlie's tenderness as well as his bewilderment over the infant, his alert, birdlike care, are highly distinctive; always that *innocence* which Charlie wore like a halo, but also an over-all purposiveness, as though the tramp knew the kid was destined to be reclaimed by his mother, later a rich opera singer, and that, as if by magic, he too would be driven away to her in the great limousine, which indeed appears instead of the patrol wagon Charlie had feared.

**111**

The limousine as a luxury symbol survives both from the days when Charlie the urchin opened the doors of carriages to resplendent theatergoers and from the unexpected re-encounter with Hetty, on that occasion seated in a luxurious auto. It is a magic vehicle which wafts him to the realization of his dream (or so he might well expect) even as a less pretentious auto comes back for him, like an unbelievable vision, in *The Vagabond*.

*The Kid* itself was a "magic vehicle" which restored him to London, where he visited the sites of his childhood and saw his mother again. Is the pattern not insistent that the mother, the child, and Charlie are a revival of Chaplin's own parental triangle in a meaningful kind of fantasy? Charlie now substitutes for his own father. Much the same thing happens to "the kid" as happened to Oedipus in that more explicit drama; he is cast off, perhaps to die, but survives and returns to his mother. Of course, in Chaplin's fantasy, "father" and "son" are amicable, are really one person. Why? Because Charlie virtually had to father himself, and to work (as, in the film, Charlie works with the kid as assistant). If Charlie is father and son, the opera singer is automatically mother and wife.

**112**

*coronation*

Intrinsically what is she, as one who becomes wealthy, but a symbol of ambiguous riches, those of sex and money combined, fluctuous as in a dream? First, she is natural wealth, the loam of the earth, as opposed to acquired wealth, money and property, and yet, since Chaplin identifies the maternal tutelage with his success, she is also the worldly riches he brings to his real mother's door as the comedian who has made good. According to the film's plot, through inheriting the kid and nurturing him, Charlie the Tramp wins the right to the opera singer and her wealth (even if he does not gain them). The mother-wife is thus the formal link between sheer work (the "art mechanism" of the desired dream) and the dream's full flowering.

The infant underdog, even as Oedipus, had to be crowned and to achieve, by whatever token, the Unattainable!

**2** 1923 was the year in which Chaplin had his mother brought to him in the United States. She was in a state of slow mental decay, and it took a great deal of courage and preparation of will for Chaplin ever to see her. She lived separately in comfort, and probably could not register reality well; it is said her main pleasure was driving with Kono, the comedian's chauffeur and private secretary, and stopping while they ate ice cream cones. There is a picture in Miss von Ulm's book showing mother and son in Hollywood, facing each other. She is rather aquiline, thick and compact in figure, and not quite Chaplin's height. She was the incarnate vestige and essence of the specter of work as opposed to its "treatment," or art (cf. Chaplin's aphorism above). She must always have seemed very distant from art, floating in its aura remotely as the inscrutable, untouchable matrix. She was brought *tragically close* only in the "short dark girls." Death erased her five years later.

1923 was also the year in which Chaplin made *A Woman of Paris,* the film starring Edna Purviance, of which, though he himself only did a bit part in it, he was the creator and director as usual. At the moment he was bringing the material vestige of his past, his mother, nearer, he was placing as far from himself as possible the vision of the

Unattainable—the "woman of Paris" (Paris: symbol of the illicit). As we shall see later, however, Chaplin was present in *A Woman of Paris* by proxy.

**3** Meanwhile, the underdog had received his worldly coronation; that is, Charlie the Tramp had doffed his famous armor, the winsome, induplicable costume, and appeared as his slender, stylish, brittle self to acknowledge the plaudits of the multitude. He repeated his visit in 1931 on the occasion of another brilliant film success, *City Lights,* and met a similar welcome.

He has told in his own book, *My Trip Abroad* (foreign title: *My Wonderful Trip*), how London came to his feet, and how with becoming surprise and intractable modesty he suddenly received a decoration from the hands of the French government. Already, in America, he had become friends with the Beerbohm Trees and with Julian Eltinge; in England, especially on the second trip, he hobnobbed with the literary and political great, meeting (at least once) Bernard Shaw, H. G. Wells,

**115**

Sir James Barrie, Lloyd George, the Duke of Windsor (then the Prince of Wales), and others. With most of them he parried in the medium of words.

Shaw reproached him with not putting enough propaganda into his films, and Barrie found fault with the plot of *The Kid*. Arguing with St. John Ervine, he found his back to the wall as he defended his position that movies should remain silent. He had to make several speeches, virtually impromptu, one of which he began with a gaff, wittily recouped, to the effect that Winston Churchill was "the late" rather than "lately the" Minister of the Exchequer; at the outbreak of laughter, Chaplin instantly revised it with "I mean the *ex*-Minister of the *Ex*-chequer." At Lady Astor's he had shocked a group of political dignitaries with a speech against modern machinery (a presage of his thesis in *Modern Times*). Lloyd George, it is said, found the comic genius boring, a posturing sort of narcissist out of costume.

The last reaction is understandable in the light of Chaplin's own book. His personality as raconteur of his European odyssey is flat, incredibly primerfied, and replete with clichés of the modest "great" . . . "I was so thrilled that all this should be happening to *me*" . . . No direct quotation, this is the provincial tone of his book incessantly, without relief, throughout; the degree of self-revelation is reduced to almost nothing. The style, whether Chaplin's own or a ghost-writer's, is hopelessly afflicted with the editorial inflection; a considerable feat, since the first-person singular begins about every other sentence.

Whatever human sighs escape from the pages of *My Trip Abroad*, whatever purple patches sprout up to decorate the "poet in words," it all manages to sound like an autobiographic serial in the very newspaper which vilified Chaplin mercilessly during Lita Grey Chaplin's divorce suit: the New York *American.*

4 *My Trip Abroad* was indeed like a real coronation ceremony, full of underplayed grandiloquence, empty of human substance on the surface, long only in the duration of its tedious strain, virtually null in retrospect, and as much a "front" for the man Chaplin as a

foreign ambassador is for the people of the nation he represents.

No doubt the trip itself was redolent with a grim triumph for Chaplin. The irony was that the hero of a dog's life (cf. *A Dog's Life,* 1918) had raised himself to the status of the uncrowned king of comedy: an emperor whose people unofficially spread over the entire globe. Another irony, somehow symmetrical and inevitable, was that Hetty the Unattainable (after having been married and widowed) had died a few weeks previous to Chaplin's arrival in London.

But all this time, Charlie the Tramp had been thriving on the distance between himself and Charles Chaplin's mother, between himself and Charles Chaplin's unattainable woman. This had constituted the professional irony of the hard-working artist: money had raised him to a point where he could do anything . . . *have* anything . . . or so it might seem. Perhaps the "distance" that made life "comic" had also fused these two feminine images, so paradoxically precious, made them into one amorphous, abstract being . . . what a philosopher has called a *far being.* This distance was in essence *un*traversible; in its midst

**118**

had sat, omnipotent, the Muse of Comedy with its tragi-comic grin, barring the grown man Chaplin and allowing to enter the past only the art-symbol, "the kid," together with his fictitious foster father, the tramp Charlie.

"The Tramp," however, was compelled to return to America with Charles Chaplin. "The kid" vanished into that lost land, the orphanage, on which, significantly, Chaplin has never conferred any of his wealth.

**5** But the coronation of the underdog had taken place only in reality, only where Chaplin was the successful little chap whose art had mesmerized a world. The fictitious "Tramp" was still a tramp, a wastrel, a misfit. His existence seemed to have a life of its own. Not only was Chaplin a dependent of "he who gets slapped," but the Tramp's private dream and social dilemma participated in Chaplin's own state of being, extended themselves without permission into his romantic longings and the realm of self-questioning that is the legacy of all who experi-

**119**

ence rage when young. And who experiences such rage? Who but the Child Aristocrat, thwarted and yoked to the world?

Chaplin could indulge his aristocratic tastes, such as they were. But his contact with men of letters and intellect made him conscious of the material defect in his personal culture. While in Europe, he began a reading course in "the classics." To be sure, he was "caught short" in more than one sense. That he could estimate the more obvious shortcomings of bourgeois society (he sympathized with Wells as to "the bunglings of democracy") and could penetrate the shallowness of society's "upper crust," is indicated by the title of *The Idle Class,* made after New York had played host to him. Here in a single title is the pith of Chaplin's envy and satire: the insistence on the *bohemian,* the *irresponsible,* the *anarchic,* that form in another social sphere the correlative of the Tramp's detached dream. How vividly this is given us in *Modern Times* when Charlie, picking up a red "danger flag" that has fallen from a truck, is accidentally caught in the path of a worker's demonstration and, swept along with them, is arrested as their leader and jailed!

A great distinction is to be made between Chaplin's *literal incarnation* of the Tramp's inveterate bohemianism, with all its pantomimic ingenuity and subtlety, and his *literary understanding* of the theme of unconventionality. The subtitles for his films were always what is known today as "corny." Naturally, one like that in *The Kid*: "Her Only Sin was Motherhood" has a broad archness that is, in a way, appropriate to the material. Yet these subtitles are but clues to the basic crudeness, unevenness, and naïveté of the great majority of Chaplin's plots. Taken apart from the intimate story of the epos I am relating here, these plots are quite negligible; that is, every one is inferior in total conception. As the world is *cold* to the Little Tramp so is it, in effect, *crude;* it is the Tramp's behavior *in a situation* that makes the world subtle. Chaplin's literary essence, in fact, must be identified bluntly as something it has remained to this day: dime-novel romanticism. His great forte has been purely theatrical: inventing situations to show off the sacrosanct qualities of the Tramp. Only through the force of a ripening complexity in his personal problem, its moral peril, did Chaplin begin (with *Modern Times*) to construct plots, however flabby, with profound ingenuities in them.

When Chaplin met the world as the great comedian, the public artist, he must have felt too much
like the inferiority of the world he somehow de-
spised. He had more respect for the Tramp and
his moronic militance than he had for his own
professional security and "medals" for achieve-
ment. Virtually, he was a "front" for the latent
genius: the fantastic waif. He—the lonely public
artist, the official genius—was a false, an inadequate realization of the Tramp's ideal. Socially
interpreted, Chaplin could see, this ideal was passive resistance and the Red Flag of the Dream:
nothing less than perfectionism. The Tramp's
technique, realistically considered, was far more
intelligent in terms of humane culture and strict
honesty than Chaplin's formal argument against
Shaw that the work of art should be evaluated in
its own terms; i.e., not as propaganda.

As I have implicitly shown in the previous sec-
tion, Chaplin was right to persist in his cheap,
Victorian sort of romanticism because this was the
ideal *emotional*, and thus esthetic, foil for simple
Charlie. . . . But his very recognition of the
Tramp's supreme moral integrity enraged his

creator: the jester's ethic was an esthetic of non-work, of *seepage* in the omnipotent, fragile dream, and a heroic acrobatics of compensation whenever the work-gesture was foisted on him. This instinctive rejection of work, which emerged as the Tramp's indispensable trait (it is like a winged lyric, a hovering Holy Ghost), is a contradiction of Chaplin's "treatment" of "work" by art. Briefly, it is not aristocratic to be an actor *unless* . . . one can act an aristocrat: *be tall, be Romeo.* . . .

**6** To the ignorance of the child, the unfamiliar actions of love may be construed as—work. I referred earlier to the communion of the parents, before which the child must exist only in a cloud of silence or secret vision. But whatever the actions of the parents, there is a period "in which the child is strictly the audience, the parents strictly the performers." If, psychologically—let us prestidigitate the vision—Charlie could replace himself with his father, then he might dream or experience some private joy with his mother which was interrupted by the privileged intrusion of his father, who would come home drunk to mother and son and appropriate his wife. This is the paradigm for the stage-box drunk annoying the music-hall performers . . . it is thus a double-faceted, a paternal-filial role.

The Tramp in the early comedies is always masquerading, and a dress suit is usually the sign of the impersonation; the element of wealth, breeding, and social station as the perquisites of the tramp's masquerade appears explicitly in *The Count* (1916). It reappears in *The Idle Class*, where as I have said a dual role exists, on one hand a real tramp mistaken for a gentleman in costume, and on the other a gentleman whose identity is temporarily obliterated by a costume, a suit of armor. "The mailed hood" has already been interpreted: it is the career-work that was metamorphosed into the tramp's costume. The two dudes in this film are identical: both are Chaplin from different emotional viewpoints; one is that in which the tramp-poet literally disguises the true Charles Chaplin and the other is that in which the tramp-poet, as *the onus of profession*, symbolically disguises the true Charles Chaplin.

124

Therefore when, as the incarnate creator of the Tramp, Chaplin experienced the Coronation of the Underdog, he was doing so *by proxy;* the crown, by essential logic, should have replaced the funny man's derby. But, by the nature of obdurate reality, it could not. This ineluctable fact did not ease, however, Chaplin's virtual misimpersonation of the Underdog when he was introduced to the Prince of Wales or to Einstein. So, like the superimposition in transparent montage, the moral-psychological perspective of a Pirandellian reality faces us. . . . On the same surface, Charlie hid Chaplin and Chaplin hid Charlie.

But the actual coronation, the feeling of being a dictator over the world of comedy miming, with the clown as minister plenipotentiary in art, created a dramatic development in Chaplin's life. His contact with the social ideas of distinguished men, particularly in 1931, intellectualized his view of himself and in a sense alienated the emotional-moral content of the Tramp. In *Pay Day* (immediately following *The Idle Class*) Charlie appears as the most realistic laborer so far exposed by Chaplin as the clown; Charlie's "normal objective" is to avoid work, flirt with the boss's daughter, and hold back his pay from his wife for "a night out." After the night out, he is caught up again in the routine of his job. Close on this, in *The Pilgrim*, Charlie is a convict who masquerades as a clergyman; patently, the oblique connotation is the hypocrisy of sanctimoniousness. But explicitly, in his pulpit, Charlie enacts the myth of David and Goliath. This objective isolation of myth in its own terms indicates progressive thoughtfulness in the comedian. Next came *A Woman of Paris*, in 1923, and then, two years later, *The Gold Rush*. This was after Chaplin had met and been married to Lita Grey . . . Of *A Woman of Paris*—later, when Monsieur Verdoux is introduced in person.

7    The social focus of *The Gold Rush* can be construed easily as the craze for money: Wall Street was then booming. But in this intimate perspective it magically revives the moment when little Charlie offered Sir Arthur Conan Doyle an equal share in their mutual incomes for the rest of their lives. The pecul-

iar coloration of this would-be pact has already been noted. Assuredly, it is a sort of over-all economic deal with the father. Coincident, in this film, with Charlie's frustrated yen for a dance-hall girl is his accidental role in helping Big Jim McKay, a gold prospector, regain his claim. Knocked on the head by a rival prospector, Big Jim loses his memory and has to get Charlie to help retrace their steps to the claim. Loss of memory is equivalent to a change of identity; indeed, both starved, the prospector imagines Charlie is a chicken and chases him with a knife: paradigm for the child's fear of the father-devourer. Desperate with hunger, they cook a shoe and Charlie goes through the pantomime of eating it, twisting the strings like spaghetti: the father in turn being eaten as well as the symbol of the great shoe: the flaw. No wonder a *pact* would be in order. As it happens, Charlie does share the gold mine and sails away rich, magnificent on shipboard in a top hat, fur-collared coat, and spats. So the proposition made to Sir Arthur was, willy-nilly, albeit symbolically, realized. And the sublime interest on the investment is the dance-hall girl hiding in the steerage.

*The Circus* intervened, three years later, between this film and *City Lights,* likewise separated by three years from its predecessor. The former's rather explicit realization of the Canio motif, its literal initiation of the waif into the professional clown's role, established without doubt Chaplin's increasing *rationalization* of his career in relation to its personal, inner complication. But *City Lights* looms as a sort of last-ditch stand of the Bohemian Poet that was the Tramp's spiritual nucleus. Aptly, the big financier, whose dipsomaniac attempt to drown himself is prevented by Charlie's appearance, emerges as a power-and-success symbol fused securely with the alter ego. After having burned up the town with Charlie, the big man, in an ecstasy of inebriated optimism, opens his heart, home, and purse to the little tramp. When sober the next day, however, he cannot remember who Charlie is and ferociously drives him out as an interloper.

The loss of memory not only links this character with Big Jim of *The Gold Rush,* thus establishing the running significance of the type, but suggests an emotional antithesis in Chaplin as the vehicle of the two egos; that is, he has two views of him-

**128**

self: when he identifies himself completely with
the power-comedian, he loathes the Little Tramp;
when he becomes drunk—a symbolic action meaning acceptance of illusion, of the Tramp's dream
—he can enter the Tramp's realm of happiness and
nourish him as Charlie himself nourished the Kid.
We glimpse the little tramp, hands clasped in
wonder and wide eyes fixed on the cash being
extended to him by the lolling, tuxedo-coated
millionaire: an unexpected gift from father to
child!

Meanwhile, Charlie is virtually fronting for the
financier as the wealthy gentleman for whom, as
we learned earlier, the blind flower girl has mistaken him when offering a posy. Charlie, as himself, befriends her and works hard to amass money
for an operation on her eyes; of course he fails.
But, returning from Europe, the millionaire gives
him the necessary money, which Charlie transmits
after much confusion. Notably, the millionaire's
being knocked on the head by a crook and again
forgetting who Charlie is, repeats the amnesia factor of *The Gold Rush* in a literal form. The girl
goes to Vienna where she gains eyesight, and Charlie disappears from her life. Later, as owner of a

flower shop, the girl encounters Charlie, fresh from a prison term, and hands him a coin, recognizing him by his touch. "You?" she falters, staring. As the film ends, we do not know whether "they live happily ever after" or not. I imagine this ambiguity about the Tramp's erotic destiny here was instinctively intended by Chaplin, since in the dimension of continuous time he could not visualize whether the Tramp's sexual ideal could indefinitely elicit monetary tribute from the millionaire comedian, so prone "to forget" in his sober arrogance. After all, a climactic and explicit burnt-offering to this ideal had already taken place with *A Woman of Paris*.

A second experience of Europe's acclaim, more talk with writers and intellectuals—and Chaplin was less sure than ever of the Tramp's future and, by corollary, of the survival of his comic alter ego's dream world. A visit with Einstein seems to have crystallized his desire to put the Tramp to work as he had never been put before. *City Lights* had been disliked by London critics as a whole. Chaplin seemed to retaliate in various unseemly ways, and his friend, Sir Philip Sassoon, gently hinted that he leave England while his general popularity was still intact. Chaplin followed his advice, but not, one imagines, without suppressed rancor. "Which one," he might well have asked, "was wearing the crown, himself or 'Charlie'?" Only *he* could completely divine the obstructiveness of the Little Tramp in the private path of the power-comedian. To others, the Little Tramp himself was Chaplin's essential triumph, complete as the lovable clown. Chaplin was jealous. . . . Where had Charlie's birthplace been? In his own heart. . . . Once more he would put him to the test, once more he would submit him—now more seriously then ever—to the crucible of the work-world, the world whose metaphysic was material wealth. Previously, in the plots of his comedies, love and money, when they had come, had come as gifts, as fairy-tale miracles. But no more!

**8** It is a credit to Chaplin's art that in *Modern Times* the stubborn waif comes out on top, for formulated more elaborately here than ever before was the concrete duel between the bohemian and the worker, between the work gesture and the dance gesture. The work-world finally becomes symbolized in a gigantic factory machine by which Charlie is accidentally swallowed and which shuttles him grotesquely about like an object of manufacture. The genius of pantomime is thus literally taken over, for the first time in Chaplin's films, by the *machine itself;* another instance in this film is the "pantomime" of the feeding machine, for which Charlie plays guinea pig, and which, as though from its own distemper, goes berserk as it feeds him. The feeding machine is not mysterious, but the great machine is a maze in which Charlie is helplessly lost and a maw which absorbs and ejects him at its arbitrary, inscrutable will. Actually it becomes a symbol of reality itself, for this is the way the real world has always treated Charlie.

By rationalization, then, Chaplin had isolated the power-world of finance capitalism into that of industrial capitalism and compelled Charlie to run its gantlet, to receive its indifference and lack of recognition, even to be mistaken for a radical and jailed. As though through the com-

*coronation*

pensation of fate, Charlie in jail inadvertently prevents a break, but while "rewarded with a comfortable cell, he is pardoned just as he is settling down to a life of ease." So even the possibility of an "illicit" comfort is invoked momentarily only in order to be shattered. It would seem that plot here is taking over some of the function of Chaplin's sadistic power-ego, while the little tramp persistently remains unreformed, while he still tends, voluntarily or involuntarily, to "wreck the works."

**9** The great machine in whose insides Charlie is temporarily trapped, swallowing and disgorging his whole body—is it not a kind of *womb*, a maternal image? As an ontological symbol of reality, it is life and death; it gives and takes. Moreover, it seems to have the moronic will of the little tramp himself, to be the *evil* counterpart of the ragged poet's *good*, if irresponsible, dream.

In these more recent films, we are dealing with

symbols more explicitly such, if still symbols emerging on the surface (as Charlie rises from the machine's labyrinth) out of the depths of the unconscious; and yet, as I have said, they were molded within as the consequence of Chaplin's increasing rationalization of his artistic and moral problem, which he more and more connected with the universal predicament of society.

The silence here is the silence of *the depths,* parallel with the depths of ocean that Chaplin had to cross twice to hear the conceptual judgments of "the great" pronounced on his work, judgments verbally conveyed. The sexual silence was always a taboo. Could Chaplin explain that primarily *this* sort of silence was his dream? He preferred the deception of the Japanese tragedian (the Tramp, too, in *Monsieur Verdoux,* was to die, although before the rise of the curtain). A sexual dream must have its strictly private character. Its remarkable dialectic, in the case of this mime, was its radical juncture with the economic problem: the necessary, immediate conversion of the *dream* into the *dream-work.* Always Chaplin's dream-work, on the surface of his life, approximated the work gesture; picture after picture had to be turned out, woman after woman met, night after night endured, kiss after kiss given—and taken back! This was the private-professional routine.

Chaplin's intellectual critics were ever urging him to consider what, in his films, he had pointed up in his subtitles: the moralistic angle, of which, thus, words were the sign. Chaplin had to reply to them, defend himself in words, in talk. But, all the while, the *verbal inarticulacy* of the tramp's dream remained its conspicuous hallmark; a dream so integral with the tramp's costume that it was the soul animating a heap of rags. What was steadily borne in on Chaplin by his intercourse with distinguished men, and by the lines of thought thus started in his own mind, was the social or suprapersonal meaning of the Tramp's figure.

It was not merely that the tramp, or rather the tramp-soul, had adventures which occurred in a virtually fairy-tale idiom, but that the "meaningful" or mythic substance of this idiom, expressed in stilted, allegorical captions and verbal labels ("The Man," "The Woman," etc.), extended the tramp's reality to the domain of all other men. Though reality appeared in simplified, hyperbolic

forms (the Policeman, for instance, representing
law and order), it did not cease to be essentially
real. Reinforced by the fact that, anyway, Charlie had always been ludicrously entangled with
reality, the pattern of *Modern Times* becomes the
most realistically coherent of all Chaplin's tramp-
laborer odysseys; its outline pattern tends toward
the *epic*. *The Gold Rush* was the first sign of the
epic; *City Lights, Modern Times,* and *The Great
Dictator,* emphasizing the epic in a rising arc, followed in logical order.

A freer, more literal "speech" was therefore increasingly required of the artist Chaplin. That the
talkies should have supervened on this problem
about the time he made *City Lights* is irony of a
transcendent kind, but not illogical or surprising
in origin, considering that his epos had been
strictly founded in the silent pantomime of early
cinema. Gestures without speech, without sound
—this was the fate of the Little Tramp; a fate ac-
cepted without protest. Silence was, finally, the
supreme armor against the reality of the world.
And yet, because a certain professional ego grew
strong in Chaplin, the hermetic silence of the
Little Tramp became hatefully irksome.

**10** Chaplin's yearning to speak the truth (i.e., "spill the beans"), which emerged so devastatingly in *Monsieur Verdoux*, first took the relative forms of placing "speech," inevitably spoken words in the talkie medium, not on the regular plane of dialogue, but making it, on one hand, *visceral*, and on the other, *transcendent* or "aerial."

The whistle which expressed Charlie's hiccoughs in *City Lights*, drawn from the realm of musical instruments, was the first literal sign of visceral speech; it is the result of involuntary factors, but nevertheless it attracts in the movie its specific audience: dogs and taxi-drivers. Does the infant in its crib not also have "involuntary" complaints which immediately attract the "specific audience" of the mother? The second example of visceral articulacy via sound was likewise involuntary and likewise sign for an infantile complaint; it is probably, in the domain of taste, Chaplin's most daring scene. It is the one in *Modern Times* when Charlie, in the hands of the police, is offered tea by an elderly female social worker,

**137**

and imbibing it, his hitherto empty stomach engenders audible gastric reactions painfully embarrassing to Charlie and the old lady. In the present pattern, the articulate viscera would stand for sexual speech, and thus, in general, for the psychic relations and their consequences.

Alas, for Charlie's simplicity! It was not so simple, no, it was not so simple. But its very genius was this: a maximum of expressiveness with a minimum of line. . . .

The love song that appears toward the end of *Modern Times,* sung to the tune of *Titina,* a popular song treating sex as comic, is not, indeed, visceral, but significantly all of double-talk. It has great charm, and assuredly it was as near as the now-gone-forever Charlie ever came to talking like his ideal, Romeo. But song is transcendent. This verbal lyricizing of love-making is contingent on Charlie's resolution to make his livelihood (he is a singing waiter) and to realize the dream-cottage he has illusorily shared with "the Gamin" (Paulette Goddard), who works in the same cafe as a dancer. The fusion of art and work in the singing waiter is as significant here as the shared dream and shared labor of the lovers; the female ideal has, like an ordinary woman, come down from her pedestal and taken her place by her man to help build their mutual future. Of course, the lovers' project fails—and for a most suggestive reason: the Gamin, being under age, is sought by the authorities, so that she and Charlie have to flee; they hit the road together, no farther along toward success than when they started. Some "flaw," some specter of the illicit, has crippled their efforts to transcend circumstance. But at least the bourgeois economic goal has become more real for followers of the Little Tramp's epic career.

That love song of Charlie's, however, given though it was in high cryptic, was not the only *transcendent* speech in *Modern Times*. There were also the first phonetic warnings of the "Great Dictator's" rantings that arrive in the factory via radio and television as the speeches of the economic boss (hint of plastic and chromium background). These speeches are at once hypocritical and lucid: their final meaning is the irrefutable command. The command to do what? Work. They represent the tyrant-overseer whose power seems remote and absolute, to operate from a higher

**139**

sphere. Not only did they represent the very ethical power Chaplin exercised over himself as the Little Tramp, but their voice, as one of command, was also that of the dead father bidding Charlie earn a living . . . strange version of the Hamlet-happening . . . yes, sound-shadow of the Ram's Horn, voice of the ancestor and the lawgiver.

There is exactly one step now to Chaplin's anticlimactic epos of *The Great Dictator,* which appeared on the surface as a satire on the triumphant Hitler, prototype of so many furious fathers: malevolent ex-sons.

**11** So exactly did Chaplin's pantomimic style as the Little Tramp fit in with the caricatured version of Hitler as Hynkel, Dictator of Tomania, that no one, to my knowledge, noticed that, in terms of comic art, Hynkel was far more in line esthetically with the Tramp than was Chaplin's other role in this film, that of the Little Barber. Again the theme of amnesia appears, and along with the double role the dramatic corollary of mistaken identity. But there are striking reorientations. Now *Chaplin*, as the Little Barber (or virtually the reformed Tramp), experiences the amnesia as result of a head wound inflicted during his service in World War I. Finally released from hospital after Hynkel's accession, he comes back to a nazified civilization without knowing what to expect. As a Jew, his shop is burned, and he and Hannah (once more Paulette Goddard), an orphan whom he has befriended, are forced to escape.

The Little Tramp, having reformed, and without the exaggerated costume or huge shoes, is less bizarre in manner as the barber, indulges in little slapstick, and seems much sobered of his intoxicating dream, which had tended to make him comatose. He is just a sentimental, humble, gentle, and blithe-spirited fellow whose hallucination is now, so to speak, only a reality whose growth, previously hidden, has suddenly overwhelmed him. Hitlerian society, now as objective as the great machine of his preceding film, is pure chimera in form and yet relentlessly substantial.

On the other hand, it is now the Dictator who

has Charlie's "intoxicating dream," a dream which, through power, he has made a reality—if a reality imposed by force on "normal" or "decent" reality. The dissolute, Nero-like drunkenness of the millionaire in *City Lights,* which was contrasted with Charlie's euphoric dream, has coalesced into Hynkel's emotional mania, into a dream of power whose *transcendent irresponsibility* has been derived from Charlie's own dream. Moreover, according to the Hitler basis, Hynkel has been an outcast, poor and persecuted, jailed and "misunderstood," even as was Charlie the Tramp. Yet a dream has driven him on—only it is an aggressive, a tyrannical dream. In this sense it is the passive—or strictly speaking *passional*—dream of the Tramp *turned inside out.*

But what characteristic of the Tramp's own dream does it perhaps retain? Internally, in terms of esthetics, it retains the dithyrambic, drunken quality, as clearly shown in the Dictator's "bubble dance," the pantomimic highpoint of the film, in which the bubble is a globe of the world; of course, in the end, like Charlie's bubble, it bursts. Externally, as applied to both Chaplin, the professional artist, and Hitler, the professional politician, the dream retains the characteristic of a transcendent power: on the one hand, artistic, and on the other, political, dictatorship. Was not Chaplin—I suggest once more—as much a dictator over the clown as Hitler was over the common man? Yet when Chaplin decided to rescue the common man from Hitler, he did so by a device for *confusing them* (mistaken identity). Previously, the victim of this device has been passive, now he turns—like the worm—aggressive. Another survival is the quasi-paternal "partner"—shadow of Sir Arthur Conan Doyle and inheritor of both the gold-prospector's and the millionaire's roles in Charlie's partitioned odyssey. Now he is in relation, of course, to Hynkel, and is no other than Napaloni (Mussolini), neighbor dictator, whom now, malevolently, "Charlie" Hynkel wants to cheat and browbeat rather than offer an equal share.

Meaningfully precise is the element of mistaken identity in *The Great Dictator*. When mistaken for Hynkel by the dictator's own soldiers, Charlie the Barber slips into the character of Hynkel the Dictator only to slip out and pronounce a speech against persecution and intolerance and, unconsciously, against himself as the creator and en-

**143**

slaver of the Little Tramp. How should this be? Because in the integument of *the only life,* which spans both art and reality, knits together the transcendent and the depths, Charlie's dream had failed in Chaplin's life—and only Chaplin the professional comedian, the art dictator, was to blame for imagining it was more than an esthetic trance. The dream had survived only amidst the abstract, semiallegorical reality in the comedian's movie fiction. Outside this, it was experiencing too vividly and powerfully the Hitlerian temptation itself: to substitute will for love, will for *being loved.* Alas, the underdog had been crowned and the crown had gone to his head. Behind the will of Chaplin, the lover, was precisely the sort of power that caused Hynkel to have his women brought before him by fiat.

That Hynkel must be the lonely unloved, that his arbitrary power—and not his image as a man —must bring, more or less voluntarily, the loved woman to bed with him, may have proved little or nothing about Hitler, but it would seem to have proved everything, or almost everything, about Chaplin's myth. It remained for the abortive masterpiece, *Monsieur Verdoux,* to prove everything beyond question. The last speech in *The Great Dictator,* in which Chaplin virtually steps out of character altogether and appears as the great little man speaking for little men who are not great— this speech indicated that, indeed, Chaplin was prepared to testify "on the stand" as to the truth of things. He did so literally at the climax of the saga of the murderous bourgeois dandy, Verdoux, and without the burlesque gibberish of Hynkel's own hilarious tirade before his people.

Hynkel had cried: "Democratia shtunk!" It is what the sly bourgeois into which the Tramp was converted in *Monsieur Verdoux* sincerely came to believe. He came to believe it as the simple-minded rationalization of the desperate democrat that the Chaplinesque Landru was.

# VI

## abdication:
### farewell with flowers

**one** Here we are, face
to face with Monsieur Verdoux, the murderous
metamorphosis of the Tramp, Chaplin's last phase.
Shall we place him in the "line-up," where indeed,
as the accused criminal, he had to stand? Is recognition possible? . . . In regard to the one actor
in the world who has remained more the same than
any other, throughout all the roles in his career,
can we say that this actor, in the spotlight of "The
Law," is really the same? But—regardless of who—
*what* is he?

**146**

**2** *Anathema.* Like Charlie, he is preposterous, but he utterly lacks inner coherence, the gesture that validates. His get-up is not born from inspiration; it is haberdashery. His elegance is thus also synthetic: consequence of the quasi-professional desire to please and a third-rate sensibility. Verdoux is a clean-cut parody of Adolphe Menjou, who acted Pierre Revel in *A Woman of Paris.* His soul is synthetic, too, being the offspring of a dismissal notice (he was originally a bank teller) and the will to hate. His delicacy of constitution is but the by-product of timidity. He is clever because he has Charles Chaplin to act him and Charles Chaplin to direct him. Otherwise, he is pathetically inept (as doubtless intended). So was Charlie. But Charlie had the transcendent gift of pantomime: an ultimate poetry of movement. Compared with Charlie's dazzling dance-antics, Verdoux's spotty choreography is that of a retired employee of Arthur Murray's, who can be persuaded to mimic Charlie chasing a dame. The only interesting thing about Verdoux is that he is part of an epos of which he apparently knows nothing. Paradoxically, his *inhumanity* is in direct proportion to his *humanization* of the Chaplin clown. He was created only, it would seem, to make a few smugly enunciated speeches that are far from being news.

**3** . . . but let us remove him from the dreadful glare of the line-up and treat him more humanly, as Chaplin desired he be treated. There is no dual role here, no mistaken identity, no amnesia (Verdoux's little address book readily supplements his lively memory), no semi-allegorical suggestion of two dimensions of reality. . . . No, only one man—and the women in his life. One man who is no longer funny, but ludicrously macabre; one man who has forgotten only that he once wore baggy pants, shoes too big, a derby and a cane, and was gloriously funny, poignantly pathetic: a child fabulously enrolling himself as *un homme de goût*. . . . One man, at least, who *wants* to forget. . . . One man who seems to remember not only what Charles Chaplin wears on the most formal of daytime occasions, but also what Menjou, as Pierre Revel, a "wealthy gentleman of leisure," wore in *A Woman of Paris*. Pierre is not only the sartorial but also the moral prototype of Monsieur Verdoux in the history of Chaplin's fictional masquerades. . . . Pierre, who has taken a village girl, Marie (Edna Purviance), on the rebound from Jean, a simple fellow to whom she has been engaged.

Turned out by her parents, who are opposed to her match with Jean, Marie plans to elope to Paris with him. But his father's death detains Jean, and, unaware of the reason for his nonappearance, Marie takes the train to Paris alone; she meets Pierre and becomes his mistress. (Is Marie not a dim symbol of Hetty, who also "did not wait"?) Pierre is thus not the hero of this "drama of fate," as Chaplin subtitled it, but the interloper, the fastidious sensual man of the world, who is the obverse, success image of the poverty-ridden, poetic tramp. It is no light circumstance that Pierre has *leisure*. Pierre is free to be himself. Chaplin had to *work at* being the Tramp.

Why didn't Chaplin want to work at his art in the way Monsieur Verdoux, fired from the bank,

takes up murder as a hard-working profession, as
packed as the life of a traveling salesman? Because in his art, Chaplin was creating merely a
myth of the frustration of a dream: the Tramp did
not have the genius of living, only that of dreaming; he did not have the genius of poetry, only that
of poetic pantomime. Part of the flaw was that
Chaplin had to *inhabit* his dream, literally wear
its "uniform," the tramp's paraphernalia, and thus
measure himself, howsoever, by the fit. Symbolically this uniform, this armor, stood between him
and his subjective ideal, the gentleman of leisure,
aristocratic and cultivated; Romeo combined with
Beau Brummell. The uniform was obstructive as
well as protective.

Pierre owned, such as it was, the pride of caste.
The Tramp, on the contrary, did not care how
much he humbled himself; he was tall in the
dream. No matter how stricken the look in the
eyes, though a kind of death lit them, the look had
the stature of the sublime—and carved in stone.
If only the Tramp had been literally (and this is a
pun) a figure of speech! The verbal quality of the
metaphor (as Proust tells us so well) is infinitely
liberating. But the Tramp's lips were sealed; his

**150**

*abdication*

shoes, leaden. As a being in a situation, as a dramatic figment, the dimensions of the Tramp's figure, and the introversive vice—the deadening
weight—of his silence, are all too visible, all too
evident as a permanent impasse. . . . Not his silence, but his silences. It was too late to begin
reading "the classics." The poet had cast his die.
The die was himself, an immature dreamer, arrested in the precocious maturity of the Child
Aristocrat, he who, though slapped, expected to
find *woman* as a gift at the foot of the manger!

4 *A Woman of Paris* is
distinguished by a solemn kind of bathos. From
the literary viewpoint, whatever its incidental vir-
tues, it is puerile. What is "a woman of Paris" in
plainer terms but the generic whore? Marie does
not have faith in Jean and subsequently yields herself to a rich man as a commodity. It was this
"gift" of a *tainted woman* which became the
Tramp's viable ideal. Elsewhere in Chaplin's films,
this same factor was customarily symbolic: the

woman's "taint" or flaw was not prostitution but
rather a quality, physical or moral, presumably
supplying the motive for—if not prostitution at
least the promiscuity of opportunism. Blindness
made the flower seller available in *City Lights*.
Social inferiority and juvenile delinquency made
the Gamin available in *Modern Times;* orphan-
hood as well as poverty made Hannah available
in *The Great Dictator;* and in *Monsieur Verdoux,*
significantly, the bank-teller's wife is available
through being crippled. As for Marie, the flaw was
possibly sublimated and abstract, but for that very
reason, being a kind of "nature" without form, it
might well be interpreted as that very empty-
headedness that makes of a woman a Trilby, a
man's "thing.". . . Chaplin's legend, in one respect, has been the history of cutting his leading
ladies down to his measure—to the moral-physical
dimensions of his own flaw. The truly unfortunate
moral is that, to play safe, to assure his own power,
he undercut it all . . . *underestimated the Tramp.*
This could only be the result of prolonged brooding on discontent, prolonged absence of secret fulfillment.

**5** The great comedian earned, and spent, millions of dollars. And meanwhile he was enchanting millions of spectators with his screen art. There was profusion in his life —profusion of glory, if you will. But the wealth was apocryphal; the fulfillment was fragmentary. A rankling will to denounce the basic conditions of life (among them, poverty) which had consigned the man to be a clown, to make the world laugh while "he was not funny really"—this will, this ingrown resentment, accumulated its capital and its sense of a destructive power; a power to destroy "the enemy."

**6** Who was the enemy? This, Chaplin has never quite been able consciously to decide, but this "identification" has cried out its mute, enigmatic pattern wherever the mechanisms of ambivalence, impersonation, amnesia, reversal, and mistaken identity have been evident in his work. Eventually, influenced by

**153**

ideas into an impersonalized form of thinking, Chaplin began to isolate "the enemy" as The Machine; i.e., as the very instrument conventionally solving the problem of poverty. But as the victimizing fate of *Modern Times,* the Machine is only the concretized, objectified principle of everything that Chaplin was as an artistic craftsman . . . *now made hideous and destructive of the human!* In the most radical and abstract sense, art is nothing but mechanism. And the perfection and humane content of Chaplin's art-mechanism never absorbed, as I have variously suggested, the whole content of reality: his own and every man's. Chaplin's irresistible genius created a great hieroglyph in the Tramp, but the clown was truly tragic enough to perceive a split in the integral fabric of life, both in himself and outside, as in a mirror; to be aware of the profound fissure of a Pirandellian dimension—the omnipresent, saturative ghost of the Alter Ego.

So "the enemy," willy-nilly, was inevitably the self, someone within, and yet the law of being is to extrovert one's evil. It is Lucifer's destiny to purge himself of self without let and without completion of the purge. The festering will of the power-comedian, millionaire in genius and money, demanded a scapegoat; some purely objective identification of the self. What was the most obvious victim? *Modern Times* tells us clearly once and for all: the Common Man, with all his naïve ideals, of which the Tramp had been the bohemian extremity, the poetic glorification; not only he who gets slapped, but also he who, in the milieu of ambiguous democracy, holds out for peace, comfort, and a home of his own—complete with radio and automobile.

Events in the world increasingly demonstrated to any valid intelligence that this dream of the common man, however individually or transiently realized, was based on quicksand—and that once removed from the magic, sacrosanct realm of Chaplin's genre comedy, the common man was the victim of a political-economic mess. So placed in the perspective of social reality, the Tramp himself, independently of Chaplin's private temperament, was ethically schizophrenic. Chaplin's steady rationalization compelled him to ask: What *tramp* does not harbor an inveterate desire to be normal, to be able to work, and gain all the rewards familiar to men: woman, children, home,

**155**

possessions, and—yes, just because he *is* a tramp—
a million dollars? What tramp has not this Alter
Ego: the implicit *would-be,* the natural *might-
have-been*?

The essential ambivalence of Chaplin's tramp-
poet character was its contradiction between the
ideal and the real, because these, formally, had
the dynamic relationship of means to end; the
ideal, that is to say, was *direct* means to the real.
The dream in the Tramp's soul translated itself
into the real without medium, and so was hallucination. Here was an echo of Rimbaud's divine
juvenile error. The Tramp was not a complete
poet. François Villon was such, but he notably
combined cutthroat banditry and the writing of
poetry without confusing them. As I have said,
Chaplin's tramp-clown had to be his own poem;
thus he could never utterly objectify the poetic.
The mute little waif, or Chaplin-Charlie, aspired
to a higher moral expression; this end-in-view was
interchangeably words and money; the conversion
of poetry into money, dumbness into articulacy.
On the plane of art, he was doomed to remain himself—as he was "at the hour of his birth"; i.e., the
child aristocrat, hopelessly frustrated; the vaga-

bond with the genius of gesture. But on the plane of reality, where *plot*, the mere pattern of dynamic existence, tended always to place him, he steadily aimed at an end which should automatically dispose of the Tramp's bohemian-pathetic style, convert him into a "new man."

Chaplin achieved his new manhood, in the overall dimension, as the successful professional who had grown up all at once to his responsibility and thereafter merely added moment to moment, dollar to dollar, film to film, without internal growth or the true liberation of the poet. So, although in this respect an existential "lag," the Tramp too grew up; as the tramp-worker of *Modern Times,* he exchanges the spontaneity of his dance pantomime, straight from the soul (how often the whole soul lay behind Charlie's single glance!) for the compulsion of mechanical gestures; in this film the work gesture becomes a rhythmic fantasy as in the animated cartoon. The art-device is morally converted into the work-device. The tramp-poet, stubborn emperor of frustration, is converted into the tramp-worker whose swan-song is the jabber-wocky love-cry at the end. The Machine had become the new master of pure pantomime.

**157**

**7** So the Machine was
the thoroughly identified enemy, the robber of art
and poetry. But we have already seen how in
*Modern Times* the machine was also a womb:
paradigm of the maternal. And the limousine: the
*luxury machine.* Woman for Chaplin, from the moment of seeing Hetty in the auto, became the
dea ex machina; high on plush, a nimbus on her
hair . . . golden. *Woman and the machine were
somehow the same.* We think of Duchamp's mechanical Bride "denuded by her own bachelors";
without friction, Duchamp's woman may fit into
Chaplin's goddess-machine. And Swinburne's image of woman as at once the mechanical plaything
and the devouring mechanism "with clockwork
joints of supple gold." Death is here, and birth
. . . and the ambushed enemy, the primordial
castration-machine.

**8** Issuing from the womb,
the infant may come too slowly, the mother may
disburse him reluctantly; somehow, if there be

"too little" of him, it might be her fault; she held back, kept some of him . . . and if she didn't, if she was generous, unselfish, she might have been too small, and could give no more than she was capable of. . . .

Hynkel is the farcical image of the child thus flawed and now furious. Is the double-talk not baby-talk? Is the bubble of the world not a child's balloon?—not the maternal breast, unmoored? Is the uniform not a child's dream of militant mastery, of the aristocracy of leisure become the dictatorship of business? But Chaplin's tendency toward realistic, objective statement logically removed the vindictive genius of Hynkel. It was enough that once he could project on a world-symbol such as Hitler his own personal power-dream and hygienically expose its absurd failure in terms of the human. Sad it is that as Hynkel, the political clown, Chaplin gave us the last manifestation of his dance genius: the elfin wizardry of movement that puts him, the child with a mustache, among the high gesturers.

But the idea of Hynkel, the preposterous dance-mime, did not go. He was the only mode left to achieve the illusion of revenge left to Chaplin the man. The practical coefficient of Hynkel's gestural style (relevant insofar as he struck the poses of a God of Power) was what? Murder. And his *speech,* somewhat like machine-gun fire, was concentrated toward nothing but murder. The dream in the Tramp's eyes had been ritually blacked out again and again. Even the tramp-worker had been victimized, become symbolic grist for the machine. Now . . . it was the turn of the puppet-master himself, the one behind the scenes, who was to project himself into art as the instrument of a predominantly *social* revenge. He was the natural descendant of Pierre Revel, elegant man about town, in the one attempt Chaplin had previously made to be realistically objective about his private-life image in terms of its success; obviously, this was when he was "really" not being "funny" but *dramatic.*

Yet the provincial naïveté of Chaplin's whole conception of *A Woman of Paris* was, as I have said, all too evident. His "realism" was devoted to touches which apparently illuminated the absurd counterpart of the serious style, implied a kind of irony, as when Pierre plays his saxophone while Marie works up a tantrum. But the irony, as cli-

*abdication*

maxed in the final "shot" when Marie and Pierre
(after Jean, in a struggle with Pierre, manages to
shoot himself) unconsciously pass each other on
the road, she in a cart, he in a limousine—this climax turns out to be bathos. The best excuse for
such inferior esthetic judgment is that Chaplin
primarily had his eye on the moral evolution of his
own nature, rather than on the work of art. In this
light, he wanted to show the "realistic" reversal of
the tramp's epos: *the man of the world enjoys the
woman and passes on, leaving her ruined.* The
ideal becomes the cast-off plaything.

**9** The truer realism of
thought that Chaplin later developed made his
private success-image pay for this symbolic triumph over "the enemy." *A Woman of Paris* was a
straying of the tramp's "depth art" into the realm
of an experimental, impersonal sort of self-flattery
—done, at all events, with mirrors. But just as Hitler, no less than Hynkel, could not be assuaged by
anything so metaphysical as flattery, "self" or

otherwise, neither could Chaplin the puppet-master of the tramp. The puppet-master had to conceive a more epic, more decisive issue. Monsieur Verdoux is merely the Frankenstein's monster of Hynkel, who remained the demoniac symbol of Chaplin.

The Tramp in *Monsieur Verdoux* is converted not only into the middle-class dandy but also into a pathological sport of sex as the murderous instrument of wealth. Here sex is strictly equated with money—that is, the adventure of sex is thus equated. The bourgeois institution of sex as respectable marriage becomes the complement, the dramatic and metaphysical foil, for sex as pure cynicism. The satirical pattern of war as murder, the thesis expressed by the words of Monsieur Verdoux on the stand and in the death cell, is but a symbolic abstraction of the real drama of sex as murder; although the dialectic link of money is common to both war and sex, money being posited here as the aim of both, the last-gasp words of Verdoux are merely a metaphysical moralism logically detached from Chaplin's personal myth. Apart from Chaplin's personal myth, *Monsieur Verdoux* is nothing but incoherence, mostly a coy variety of bathos. For the argument that war is business, and that this is its crucial meaning, can be demolished by the observation that *the common man* is the prime instrument, the indispensable robot, of war, and that *his* are not the profits. Monsieur Verdoux is the apostolic zombi, not of the business of war, which is the weak moral excuse, but of a philosophy of violence, causally to be validated only by reference to the laws of the libido and their social fates, not to those of capitalist enterprise and their military fates. Is it possible that Chaplin is being a devious joker and (trapped with a catch in his voice) is asking public opinion to forgive him his sex-trespasses as it forgives the war-trespasses of the capitalists? I wonder. . . .

**10** Money in Chaplin's calamitous film is the symbolic coefficient of a sexual charm held in very disproportionate degrees by Verdoux's successive victims and near-victims. Ostensibly, Verdoux's crippled wife and their child, ensconced in a home obviously paral-

leling the dream-cottage of *Modern Times,* provide the "efficient cause" of the tin-whistle dandy's maneuvers in the field of murder. The
knowledge that marriage, the identical act of coi-
tion, takes place at least once with each of the
little murderer's intended victims, renders dis-
gusting not only these acts but also the acts of sexual consummation with Verdoux's bona fide wife.
The perfunctory gestures which Verdoux goes
through at home, however, as obviously a satire
on the humdrum nature of middle-class life, indicate that a pervasive *formalism* in sex is Verdoux's
natural characteristic. By this very token, his relations with the illegal wives he plots to murder
take on a strictly substitutive or symbolic role. One
has no way of knowing in what sense Verdoux's
sexual relations exist either at home or abroad.
Astonishingly enough, the thought breaks in that
these relations are as fully chimerical as were the
strictly ideal relations of the Tramp during *his*
frustrated moments.

The elliptical bohemianism of Verdoux's strange
morality is evident. His lethally cynical tactics
have the same intrinsic promiscuity as daydream-
ing, with the difference that the absolute sex act

was necessary to the logic of the Tramp's beautiful dream, whereas sex's trumpery, meaningless shadow, is all that is involved with Verdoux's practical dream of murder profits which, when realized, he promptly invests. Verdoux, the dapper little man who confronts us so shockingly, chiefly because he seems like Chaplin himself as commonly portrayed off screen, emerges as the strict bourgeoisifying of the Tramp. Identically, the Tramp and Verdoux are adventuristic, lone-wolf, and pathological in character-pattern—although that isn't all the Tramp is.

What is the chief difference between Verdoux and Charlie, the once supreme? Verdoux is devoid of heart and, not surprisingly, also of the poetry of pantomime. He maintains the tradition of the clown's wit—yes, and now *verbalized* by the man forced to parry with Shaw or Barrie in literary argument—but it is a wit that kills leadenly, humorlessly, without sparkle or the grace of irony. Seldom does Chaplin as Verdoux even approximate the physical dance-grace of Charlie; such demonstrations as enter the plot are rather pale replicas, indeed much like rehearsals of the real thing, with the actor not in costume but in his

**165**

regular clothes. Having been deprived of heart (save in an irrational access of feeling, of which later), and correspondingly of costume, the Tramp now bears a strong family resemblance to Chaplin the private individual. Did Chaplin ever put on the screen an image so literally his own? Patently, never.

Money is a substitution for the sexually desirable in that, since ostensibly these women do not have what Verdoux desires (assuming he can honestly desire anything sexual), he prefers to elicit from them money rather than the love act. Now it is quite possible to relate this explanation to the common man as substitutive sex-robot. But psychological investigation has told us that, in the extreme form in which this robotism and substitution appear in Verdoux, it is nothing but the adult pathology of infantilism, the equivalent in infantile life being the emotional exchange with the mother, including exchange of actual caresses; that is, candy and other gifts may become substitutes for kisses and embraces.

Pierre Revel as inheritor of chivalric ideals has acquired in his incarnation as Verdoux some of the vitiated characteristics of the women he has kept, the complexion, to be specific, of the "generic whore." Verdoux is an aggressive variety of prostitute, a "workhorse" version of the gigolo. He does not, it should be noted, locate some Madame Grosnay (one of his intended victims), a woman of refinement and style as well as money, and, seducing her, become her fixture. No, he is not realistic or simple enough—one might even say "normal enough." He has to keep in his life the empty symbol of respectability, the moral consolation of being a "good woman's support" and the father of "future citizens." Thus Verdoux, far from being a libertine, is a petty-bourgeois prig with a pathological streak of violence, and only in the least funny because of his lack of skill and ultimate proficiency. He is like the lowest variety of streetwalker who has to chase customers. This is the "comedy" of *Monsieur Verdoux*.

Another link with the Little Tramp appears: Verdoux's practical ineptitude. The device of the chain-murder plan is only a prodigal effort to overcome an ineluctable weakness, secreted firmly in the self. This expresses itself in the lack of straightforward aptitude and skill in terms of work. So failure and final apprehension of the

**167**

murderer are inevitable. Verdoux makes a point of giving himself up, even though, in the manner of Chaplin's early comedies, fate smiles on the frantic little fugitive by offering him a momentary hole of escape. It is impressive that his decision to toss up the sponge is not only the result of the post-war depression in the murder business, and the death of his wife and child, but more persuasively, because he has been recognized. So (while in a restaurant where he has gone to dance with a certain lady) he suspects from the horrified glances of a thin old crone at one of the tables; he is right, as we know, and it is not long before the police arrive. In a sense, he has only been waiting for this identification. That he does not go away with the certain lady but gives himself up seems a token that he is identified as more than the man who has murdered the sister of his accuser. For he is identified as a *vagrant,* as permanently out of the murder business; yes, as ghost of the doorstep haunter, the slum duke, the ashcan Merlin: *the Tramp!*—and he is identified as still more.

**11** As a matter of fact, he has already been identified by the lady he has gone to dance with, a girl whose life with unique volition he once spared, as that prototype: Hetty's onetime lover, *the man on the curb whose eyes raise themselves to the woman in the limousine.* . . . For now this girl, exactly as the real-life Hetty and as the fictitious heroine of *A Woman of Paris*, has risen in the world through making a "profitable connection"; husband or lover, it does not matter which: he has given her a limousine. The little man on whose forlorn figure her eyes descend from it receives that exquisite, unique thrill so often registered by the Tramp when he saw his vision. She is mysterious and somehow unattainable; and, like the woman of Paris, an ambiguous taint seems to qualify her; in some manner, she has "sold" herself. It is implicit that, at this moment of recognition, what might make her available— among all the things that have made Chaplin's heroines available—is the consent to be promiscuous, to "sell out," but meanwhile fate has intervened and caused her to accept a previous opportunity.

**169**

Since their first meeting, the tables have been turned. Verdoux, conducting a going business, picked up a tall, pretty, bedraggled girl from a rainy doorway and asked her to his room in order to submit her to a poison experiment. After hearing her story, however, he changes his plan and gives her money because he learns that she loves a cripple—even as he, supposedly, loves a cripple, his wife. It is not necessary that her love be passionate, romantic, truly sexual; it must merely be, as it seems, self-sacrificing. At this time, the fabulous dea ex machina, while available as a derelict, has already committed herself to someone who—like Verdoux, like the Tramp, and like Chaplin himself—has a "flaw." Verdoux, the man of the moment, cannot be *the* one simply because she has already made a choice. Moreover, ostensibly and according to his own self-estimate, he is not himself crippled, for he, like the girl, has sacrificed himself for a flawed individual. So his identification as the one destined for the goddess' smile was formally impossible at the moment he withdrew the poisoned wine from the girl's reach. As she is a *dea*- he is a *deus* ex machina. The process has been almost mathematical. The Tramp is now

**170**

_Note:_

_abdication_

finally equated with—cut to the measure of—the Ideal Woman as, with the tour de force of art, Chaplin had equated himself with all the women of his life. Nor, identified from the limousine, can the second meeting with the goddess make Verdoux the choice because she has met an arms manufacturer and is now mistress of his wealth. . . .

If Verdoux is a version of the Tramp, it seems to me that the two unseen men in the film, the cripple and the millionaire successively chosen as objects of the girl's favor, are both essentially Chaplin transposed to the realm of pure fiction. Chaplin identifies himself with these imaginary men because they have been "lucky" enough to gain such a prize: the tall, lovely blonde. They are unseen stereotypes for, first, the _Charlie_ for whom Edna returned in _The Vagabond_ and, second, the _Pierre_ who garnered the hard-up _Marie_ in Paris. . . . Peripety, reversal, recognition. . . . In this classic manner, Chaplin took care of his love epos and finally chose a form for it which should place the alter egos in an order joining first one and then the other to the Woman of the Vision, but leaving his third character, Verdoux, outside.

**171**

**12** The third, Verdoux, sticks out like sore reality itself. He was not only literal symbol of the diehard dictator, but also the reincarnation of Chaplin's primitive role of the Property Man, malapert disrupter of the art-fiction from behind the scenes. . . . In this latest movie, women are the "properties" and the "art-fiction" is the Tramp's dream of true love. If Chaplin had indeed reached the heights as loyal interpreter of this wordless dream, if he had had the illusion of loving truly in life as the Tramp loved truly in fiction, this did not dispose of the guilt that had long inhered in him and festered grievously.

. . . and the guilt is *what*? The arrogance of a make-believe not in terms of art but in terms of life, and the mechanical, diurnal submission to this arrogance; in short, a ritual moralistic belief in something less intrinsically true than the Tramp's dream: the real dream of power deposing the fictitious dream of love. Chaplin was guilty of accepting *life* as a mechanism, and in it, as in the Great Machine of *Modern Times,* Charlie the Tramp was a helpless pawn.

**172**

**13** *"Killing is a form of our wandering sorrow"*—Rilke. Chaplin was caught up in the mechanism of the contingent social morality that capitalistic democracy too is a big, bad machine, the only valid attitude toward which is to attempt to master it (like Verdoux) through guile and at any price. This is the power psychology typical of dictatorship. Verdoux is Hynkel's genius disguised as a bank teller who enters "sex speculation"—a remote branch of Wall Street. His softness is the reflex of strategy, the gift for survival. Irony is supposed to be his objective quality. A little man, he murders in big only from his end of the telescope (cf. "life viewed from a distance" above). The paradigm for him, as the opening garden scene shows, is the insect: a male mantis in revolt against the pitiless female, irresistible, dualistic machine of sex and murder. He has a game to outwit her; it can work only conditionally, when destiny is not on the alert in applying her rules.

It is not that Chaplin, in his medium of Verdoux, could not dimly recognize his own fate—it is that he has never done so directly, completely. The Tramp's lack of familiarity with speech seems to have given Chaplin a proportionately exaggerated faith in it. It becomes an emotional and intellectual vice: the magic key to every problem. The Tramp's transcendent speechlessness, the negative emblem of his genius, seems to exist in Verdoux's past as a form of aphasia; a natural concomitant for pathological murder. Like other pathological murderers, Verdoux gives himself up out of the masochistic urge to confess. As in one suffused with guilt, the miracle of speech occurs. He can speak at last . . . or, in terms of gesture, *spill the beans.*

**14** But that Chaplin himself considered his film only a relative, inadequate form of the truth should be illuminating. Verdoux in his death cell is not in the least pathetic or moving, thus not convincing. He is a man in his shirtsleeves delivering to the world his message of guilty self-exoneration while under the illusion of being noble: as "noble" as he dare be.

**174**

### abdication

This message too is double-talk, far more profoundly obscure in all its elementary grammar than the scintillant gobbledegook of Charlie the singing waiter. For it screens all the private man. Politically, this message is the most old-fashioned of late nineteenth-century platitudes, having been crystallized once and for all by Marx. That it should be exploited in this way is constructive only as it concludes the epos of the most amazing of underdogs.

The crown of the underdog was made of words; they went to his head. Alas, the dictator type is one which acquires its inferiority under the presumably inflexible, insuperable conditions of democracy, and which wreaks its destiny by this theoretical compulsion. The moment of voluntary abdication in *The Great Dictator* (as the result of the mistaken identity) is repeated in *Monsieur Verdoux,* but here the identification of the abdicator is correct: he is the underdog giving up the ghost. The respective speeches are diametrically opposed in content, the old one expressing hope for a democratic future, the new one an utter submission to worldly fate. The *social universe* has become the demoniac machine. . . .

**175**

But think of the little man we first see clipping roses while the chimney of his villa in the background disgorges the smoke of his late wife. The blood which this hypocritical nursemaid of caterpillars has on his soul is nobody's, nobody's really, but Charlie's. True, we do not witness a murder of this sort. And if we did, if it *were* such an honest murder, it would probably reverse the roles of killer and killed.

Like Deburau pining away after the unresponsive statue of the goddess in *Les Enfants du Paradis,* Charlie might have vented himself on Chaplin the way the French mime as Pierrot (fulfilling the deadly violence of the clown's tradition) beats to death the clothes-mendicant whom he cannot pay. It is the displaced passion of Eros with which Pierrot kills. Praising *Les Enfants* as "a very beautiful and extraordinary story," Chaplin must have perceived a distorted analogy between Deburau-Pierrot's terrifying, aggressive passion and Chaplin-Charlie's mute, submissive passion. When Verdoux was born from the monolithic matrix of the power comedian, Charlie's supernatural gentleness was crucified in the depths of Charles Chaplin.

**176**

**15** *"The Tramp is dead."*
—Chaplin. In a way we have Chaplin's own word
for it all. The sentence is a less decorative report
than the sort furnished in Greek tragedies and
quite without the death-agony visible in Japanese
tragedies. We do not, assuredly, see the swords go
into Charlie, nor do we witness his "upward" death
in "the most bew-tiful movements you could see."

Recall! Charlie's deaths were comic deaths,
sham deaths. The blunt blows he received were
instruments of the comatose, holding in their
hearts the genius of the dream. These blows (like
the one he inflicted on himself as Carmen's Don
José) resurrected as they killed. His dance of
death rhymed with claps of laughter. At the beginning of Verdoux's death march, the murderer
turns his back to the camera. The gesture is in
good taste. But the economy of line is crushing,
the silence leaden, the dignity redundant, the silhouette uncommunicative. . . .

**16** I have virtually declared that one member of the ego pair murdered the other. I was prepared to reiterate it, to lament Charlie's loss, and to say, "Genius is dead"; perhaps write an elegy. But can genius die and leave its "other"? Does it not persist by whatever means? Does it not by its very nature transcend the human ego in which it is lodged? My hand was wrapped in black, my fingers poised over the typewriter keys . . .

Reversal, peripety . . . Perhaps Chaplin has become an altogether unconscious master of these. I have said that Verdoux was the descendant of Hynkel, and Hynkel the segregation of Chaplin's malice and dream of power; in a way, "Charlie Verdoux" went back to Hynkel, as Hynkel revived the dionysian Tramp. The action of the telescopic may be involute; ends are sometimes rebirths; one can begin at the end and go back toward the beginning. Does this power lie in Verdoux's ashes? Are they perhaps not those of the phoenix? If Verdoux be a kind of matrix . . .

. . . then: yes, he might be the rebeginning of

**178**

the cycle. Precisely! He dies. He gives up. But he does so as a common man with symbolically common guilt; as Chaplin would have died, would have given up, *had he been a common man.* But let us presume Verdoux concealed more than one possibility in his dudish person; let us assume this possible ego was as desperate as Verdoux but that he did not have Verdoux's vulgar adventurism, that he rejected the idea of victimizing women; that he was constrained to leave home and family, say farewell to the actual dream cottage, and become—not a murderer—but the *genesis* of Charlie the Immaculate.

I say: Charlie, perhaps, was *not* born full-blown; that he had a past like anyone else. I say that it might have been a past somewhat like Verdoux's beginning of the end: symbolically the utter bourgeois disillusionment, the moral catharsis and lyrical rebirth. I say that Chaplin's epos (and how heartening is this farewell thought!), if viewed logically rather than chronologically, may contain Verdoux's moral experience somewhere at the beginning of his life, and that it gave birth to the heavenly Tramp, triumphing over the materialistic devices of the pathological. Add genius to

Verdoux's misfortune and you have the formula for the future Tramp! The fantastic costume is the parody of Verdoux, who is a parody of Pierre Revel. A parody elevated by absolute poetry and the glory in the heart of a child.

If, historically, the Child Aristocrat thus triumphed, not in rage, but in gentleness and poetry, Verdoux is a throwback. If Verdoux was reborn, his mother was Necessity, not Art. If his father was Chaplin—who else?—it was Chaplin kissing his youth good-bye.

Verdoux is . . . how Charlie came to be.

# A PORTFOLIO
## OF CHAPLIN PHOTOGRAPHS
### 1914–1947

2. 1918. (THEODORE HUFF)

1. 1914 (age 24), as he looked when he entered the movies. (THEODORE HUFF)

CHARLES CHAPLIN: METAMORPHOSIS FROM THE "IDEAL ROMEO"

TO THE "IDEAL MAN OF THE WORLD."

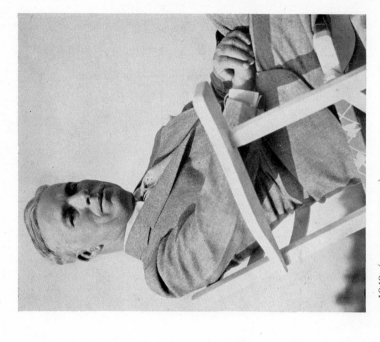

3. 1925. (THEODORE HUFF)

4. 1940. (THEODORE HUFF)

5. Charlie as female impersonator: identification with the love-object. (THEODORE HUFF)

6. Charlie in the image of the gentleman-drunk: disrupter of "the show." (JOSEPH CORNELL)

7. Edna elicits the early love-look from Charlie: the poet's trance. (JOSEPH CORNELL)

8. Charlie's perennial squabble with massive man. (JOSEPH CORNELL)

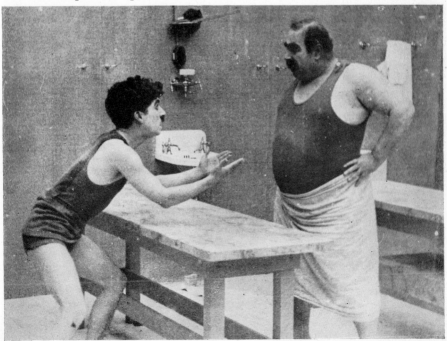

9. The huddled soul of the waif looks up: the clown's infinite sadness. ( JOSEPH CORNELL )

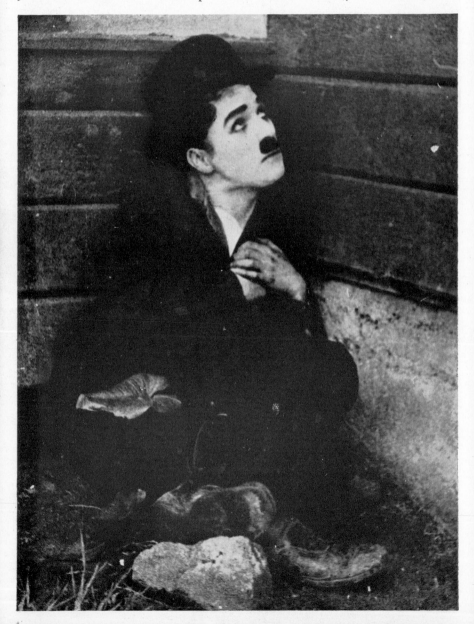

10. Charlie à la Nijinski in a classic pose; Chaplin's rhythmic, routine "business" as the clown was more like the later, "modern" Nijinski: fluid, precise, staccato movement. (THEODORE HUFF)

11. Revival of childhood: the man as child and the child as man via the famous silhouette. (This still is from the early sequence of *Shoulder Arms*, never included in public showings of that film.) (THEODORE HUFF)

12. Love: the transforming power of music. (THEODORE HUFF)

13. Chaplin at work with Jackie Coogan reviving his past: note the sweetness and simplicity of Chaplin's casual expression. (JOSEPH CORNELL)

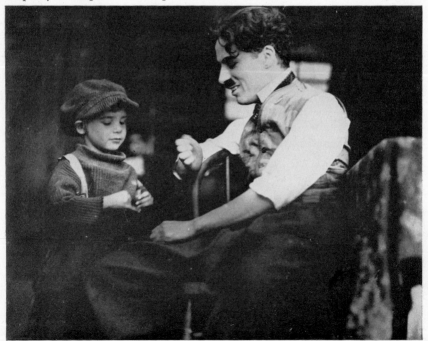

14. Millionaire in mufti: the love-look is never disguised. (THEODORE HUFF)

15. Arabesque on high: the tramp's angelic poise (while clowning offstage). (JOSEPH CORNELL)

16. The paternal partner comforts the child-tramp.

(THEODORE HUFF)

17. Chaplin, *au naturel*, concentrating on *A Woman of Paris,* an exclusive starring vehicle for Edna Purviance; he directed it, but appeared in it only fleetingly as a porter. (JOSEPH CORNELL)

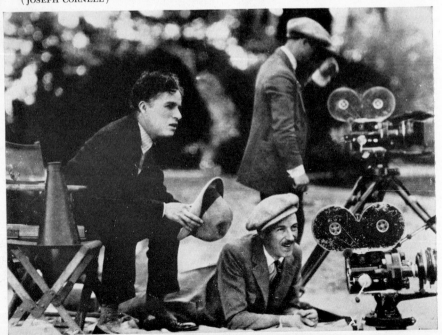

18. Charlie as the blind flower-seller's illusion: a great gentleman.
    ( JOSEPH CORNELL )

19. The millionaire ex-tramp gazes at the fetich-image of the Ideal. ( THEODORE HUFF )

20. Charlie's most ambiguous expression—the master comedian invents an emotion on the spur of the moment for a publicity "still." (THEODORE HUFF)

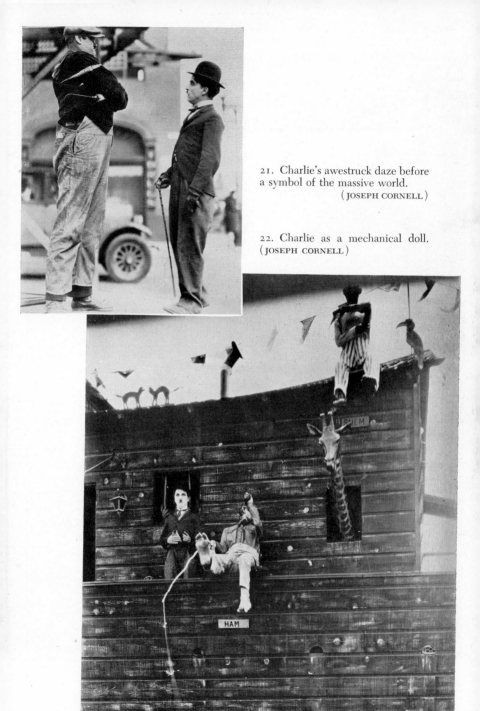

21. Charlie's awestruck daze before a symbol of the massive world.
(JOSEPH CORNELL)

22. Charlie as a mechanical doll.
(JOSEPH CORNELL)

23. The reformed tramp and his girl-friend apply for a job. (JOSEPH CORNELL)

24. Charlie being nonchalant in front of the Great Machine. (JOSEPH CORNELL)

25. Love-mania of the Tramp into hate-mania of the Dictator. (THEODORE HUFF)

26. "Monsieur Verdoux": the final mask. (UNITED ARTISTS)